HEALTH COOKBOOK
FOR FAMILY AND FRIENDS

HEALTH COOKBOOK
FOR FAMILY AND FRIENDS

By Cory SerVaas M.D. and Charlotte Turgeon

The Saturday Evening Post Society
Indianapolis, Indiana

Design by JMH Corporation, Indianapolis

Jean White, Editor
Robert Wathen, Proofreader
Phyllis Lybarger, Compositor
Vince Cannon, Layout Artist

Published in Nashville, Tennessee, by Thomas Nelson, Inc., and distributed in Canada by Lawson Falle, Ltd., Cambridge, Ontario.

Printed in the United States of America.

ISBN 0-8407-3135-3

TABLE OF CONTENTS

INTRODUCTION

If you love your family and friends, it's a challenge for the 1990s to stay abreast of the fast-breaking information about food choices that can help us to avoid degenerative diseases and even malignancies.

In this collection of recipes Charlotte Turgeon has made the transition to a low-fat, low-cholesterol, low-salt diet an exciting culinary experience. Included are unusual seasoning and serving suggestions that owe much to Charlotte's long residence in France. The recipes call for healthful American ingredients but combine them as a Parisian chef might.

Today's thoughtful hostess—our super hostess or super mom—doesn't keep guests in the dark about which dishes presented will violate their diets. There are many easy ways to do this. Our hostess thinks ahead and might consider the following ideas:

She may go all the way with a computer printout listing all the ingredients in her tempting party dishes. She probably keeps her recipes on a computer anyway, so printing the recipes to go with her party menu for the guests is not really a chore. She keeps the recipes updated as more detailed information about diet and health becomes available. Saturated fats are replaced with polyunsaturated or monounsaturated fats. Olive oil becomes a favorite, and of course it is announced to the guests. Guests are told that egg whites or egg substitutes are used instead of whole eggs. Guests are told that herbs and spices are substituted for sodium chloride. Oriental dishes made without monosodium glutamate are announced in the presentation to guests. At the end of the meal, extra copies of recipes are readily available for interested guests.

In the wake of the Alar scare, organically grown apples seemed worth the effort to some cooks. If their apple pies were made with insecticide-free apples, they let their guests know that.

If your carrots are organically grown, the flavor will say so. Tasting the organically grown carrot is a treat. Good cooks we know are paying attention to organically grown produce because of its superior flavor.

When you invite guests to dinner, it is thoughtless to serve a meat dish to a vegetarian unless there was no way of discovering that your guest doesn't eat meat. A phone call in advance can often reveal important food preferences or diet requirements. If your grandmother can no longer digest the gluten in wheat, make sure some rice muffins are available for her.

If one of your party revelers is pregnant, make sure there is some non-alcoholic bubbly for her if there are to be toasts. If a guest had PKU as a child, and might be pregnant or even about to become pregnant, make sure all vestiges of NutraSweet products are removed from your menu.

If you have guests who are fighting cholesterol, you'll be sparing them concern if you let them know that there's no coconut oil, palm oil, or other highly saturated fats in your recipes.

Don't assume your guests are willing to forget their calorie counting, or their healthy heart food regimen, just because *you're* giving a party. Special days come often for busy people, but they no longer find birthdays or holidays an excuse for blowing the diet. The birthday cake, the wedding cake, the ham on New Year's Day—these are outmoded traditions that need replacing. It's time for some of us to weed out the unhealthy recipes in our files and initiate our own new family traditions more in tune with the times.

Pioneers aren't always popular—we won't tell you it would be easy to get rid of the Christmas candy-laden gingerbread house if your mother has been making one for her children or grandchildren for the past forty years. But delectable holiday substitutes can be improvised to scuttle her candy display. She's probably so busy assembling these sweet health hazards that she doesn't have time to get in for her yearly mammogram, so get her out of the kitchen for that. Then encourage her to arrange beautiful fruit bowls when she has no time left for the candy gingerbread house.

You no longer need sacrifice your principles when you entertain. If you don't permit smoking in your home, your friends and relatives should know this, and when they accept an invitation, they will come prepared to step outside if their addiction demands an after-dinner cigarette. You no longer need fear being branded a crusader just because you protect your guests from having to suffer unwanted tobacco fumes.

If you travel in Switzerland, Italy, or many other European countries, you can stock up on nonprescription Nicorette to share with your smoker friends who would rather chew it than offend other guests by smoking. Nicorette is still a prescription drug in this country, but that is probably so that doctors will have a chance to help counsel the user into quitting. It is certainly far less dangerous than cigarettes. Just sucking on a piece of Nicorette can politely deliver a "nicotine fix" to the veteran smoker, your guest doesn't get "antsy" to sneak out for a cigarette, and you may have started him on the road to freedom from the dangerous habit.

I trust that this book will help you to plan many happy occasions when family members and friends can share good food and good fellowship around your table without endangering their health. Bon appétit.

Cory Servaas, M.D.

Basic Recipes

Chicken Broth
Cornstarch Milk
Whole-Wheat Cream Sauce
Vinaigrette
Italian Dressing
Low-Calorie Mayonnaise Dressing
Low-Fat Green Mayonnaise
Creamy Herb Salad Dressing
Boiled Salad Dressing
Simple Tomato Sauce
Pesto
Duxelles
Whole-Wheat Crepes
Soufflé Pancakes
Lo-Chol Pastry
Honey Cheese Cream
Whipped Dessert Topping
Three-Grain Refrigerator Bread or Rolls
Multi-Grain Food Processor Bread

"Who told you spinach was loaded with cholesterol?"

CHICKEN BROTH

Chicken broth is basic to all kinds of cooking and should be made in quantity and stored in convenient amounts in your freezer. Ask the butcher to get a five-pound package of chicken backs, necks, and wing tips from his supplier or, better yet, get several packages so that you will have some on hand in case your supply runs low unexpectedly.

5 pounds chicken backs, necks, and wing tips	Handful of parsley
6 quarts water	1 bay leaf
2 onions, sliced	3 sprigs thyme
2 carrots, sliced	1 lemon, sliced
4 stalks celery	1½ teaspoons vegetable seasoning
	8 peppercorns

Put the chicken in a large soup kettle. Add the water and bring slowly to a boil, skimming off the froth that rises to the surface. When the froth is diminished, add the rest of the ingredients and simmer 2½ hours. Let the chicken pieces cool in the broth. Strain the broth. Strain the broth again through a sieve lined with a double thickness of dampened towel. Refrigerate overnight to allow all the fat to congeal at the top.

The next day remove all the fat. Divide the broth into containers and freeze. Do not season the broth more until you use it. This allows for a greater variety of uses.

• • •

CORNSTARCH MILK
Yield: 1 pint

Texture is very important to good menus no matter what the dietary restrictions. Cornstarch milk, which is low in calories and cholesterol, gives texture to soups, sauces, and custards. The "milk" requires cooking, but once prepared it will keep in the refrigerator for several days.

1 pint low-fat milk

2, 4, or 6 tablespoons cornstarch

Fill the bottom of a stainless steel double boiler with enough water to touch the bottom of the top part. Bring the water to a boil and heat 1 cup of milk in the top part until it starts to simmer. Whisk the cornstarch into the remaining cup of cold milk until smooth. Two tablespoons will make a thin sauce, 4 tablespoons will make a medium sauce and 6 tablespoons will make a thick sauce. Whisk the mixture into the hot milk and cook, whisking frequently, for 5 to 10 minutes or until thickened. Cover and cook 10 minutes longer over simmering water; this will remove the gritty taste of cornstarch. Strain and cool. Cover and keep in the refrigerator.

•   •   •

WHOLE-WHEAT CREAM SAUCE
Yield: 1½ cups

This is the base of many sauces—parsley sauce, cheese sauce, onion sauce, green onion sauce, and many others. Frozen cream sauce is a convenience. Whisk it well while reheating, since it tends to separate.

3 tablespoons unsalted
    polyunsaturated margarine
4 tablespoons whole-wheat
    pastry flour

1 cup low-fat milk
¼ teaspoon salt substitute
    (optional) and/or 1 teaspoon
    lemon juice

Heat the butter or margarine in a small saucepan. Whisk in the flour. Reduce the heat and whisk over moderate heat for 2 to 3 minutes. Do not brown.

Add the milk and whisk until thickened. Remove from the heat and add the seasoning.

. . .

VINAIGRETTE
Yield: 1 cup

1 teaspoon Dijon mustard
¼ teaspoon salt substitute
    (optional)
⅛ teaspoon freshly ground
    black pepper

⅓ cup red or white wine
    vinegar
⅓ cup olive oil
⅓ cup peanut oil

Place all the ingredients in a jar. Cover tightly and shake until blended. Chill

in the refrigerator. Shake again just before using.

. . .

JEANNE

ITALIAN DRESSING
Yield: 1½ cups

2 large basil leaves
½ cup vegetable-tomato juice
¼ cup red wine vinegar
¼ teaspoon salt substitute
   (optional)

⅛ teaspoon freshly ground
   black pepper
⅔ cup olive oil

Spin the basil leaves with the tomato juice, vinegar, seasoning, and 1 tablespoon of the oil in a food processor. While still spinning, slowly add the remaining oil so that it emulsifies and thickens. Pour into a jar and chill before using.

•   •   •

LOW-CALORIE MAYONNAISE DRESSING
Yield: 1 cup

½ cup 1%-fat cottage cheese
2 tablespoons skim milk
½ cup light (reduced-calorie)
   mayonnaise
1 teaspoon lemon juice

Optional additions:
1 tablespoon freshly chopped
   Italian parsley
1 tablespoon minced chives
2 teaspoons chopped pimiento

Purée the cottage cheese and milk until smooth. Add the mayonnaise and the lemon juice and blend well. Keep in a covered jar in the refrigerator.

•   •   •

LOW-FAT GREEN MAYONNAISE
Yield: 2 cups

2 cups fresh spinach leaves
  Small bunch watercress
  Small bunch parsley
4 scallions (white and green
  parts)
1 medium-size fresh cucumber
¾ cup low-calorie
  mayonnaise dressing

¾ cup plain yogurt
1 tablespoon white wine
  vinegar or lemon juice
  Salt substitute or vegetable
  seasoning (optional)
⅛ teaspoon white pepper

Place the spinach and watercress leaves in a strainer and place it in rapidly boiling water for 1 minute. Remove, drain thoroughly, and cool. Chop the leaves, parsley, and scallions by hand or in a food processor using the on-off switch. Do not purée. Wash and halve the cucumber. Scoop out the seeds with a spoon. Dice the unpeeled cucumber. Combine the chopped greens, the mayonnaise, the yogurt, the cucumber, the vinegar or lemon juice, and seasoning if desired. Mix well and place in a covered jar. Use within two days.

•   •   •

9

CREAMY HERB SALAD DRESSING
Yield: 1 pint

2 tablespoons chopped
  parsley
2 tablespoons chopped chives
½ teaspoon chopped fresh
  thyme
1 teaspoon chopped fresh
  basil
1 cup low-fat cottage cheese

1 cup yogurt
1 large clove garlic, pressed
1 teaspoon lemon juice
½ teaspoon salt substitute
  (optional)
¼ teaspoon freshly ground
  black pepper

Chop the parsley, chives, thyme, and basil in a food processor. Add the cottage cheese and spin until smooth. Add the yogurt, garlic, lemon juice, and seasoning. Spin 1 second and pour into a jar. Cover and refrigerate.

•   •   •

BOILED SALAD DRESSING
Yield: 1½ cups

2 tablespoons cornstarch
1 teaspoon dry mustard
⅛ teaspoon paprika
½ cup water
2 tablespoons cider vinegar

4 tablespoons unsalted
   polyunsaturated margarine
⅔ cup skim milk
1 packet artificial sweetener
1 cup plain yogurt (optional)

Mix the cornstarch, mustard, paprika, and water. Cook over low heat until thickened. Stir in the vinegar and margarine, and gradually add the milk, cooking until creamy. Remove from the stove and add the sweetener. For variation add 1 cup of yogurt and whisk until blended.

•   •   •

SIMPLE TOMATO SAUCE
Yield: 3 cups

1 cup chopped onion
2 tablespoons olive oil
1 quart canned tomato purée
   (unsalted, if available)
2 cloves garlic, pressed
1 bay leaf
½ teaspoon thyme

½ teaspoon oregano
⅛ teaspoon sugar
2 tablespoons chopped
   parsley
   Freshly ground black
   pepper
   Salt substitute (optional)

Sauté the onions in the olive oil until soft and shiny. Stir frequently. Add the remaining ingredients, except for the salt substitute. Simmer covered for 30 minutes. If the sauce seems too thin, remove the cover and cook down to desired thickness over higher heat, taking care that the sauce does not scorch. Remove the bay leaf and season to taste.

•   •   •

PESTO
Yield: 3 cups

A little pesto goes a long way and makes a wonderful seasoning for vegetables as well as for pasta. Pesto can be frozen in small containers and used as needed.

1 cup (well-packed) fresh basil
   leaves
6 cloves garlic, pressed
½ cup grated Romano cheese

½ cup grated Parmesan cheese
¼ cup pine nuts or walnuts
2 cups olive oil

Put the basil, garlic, cheeses, and nuts in a food processor and process to a smooth paste. Add the oil gradually through the feeder tube.

•   •   •

DUXELLES

*Duxelles is a basic mushroom concoction that is used often in
French cooking in all kinds of entrée preparations. It is easy to make in
large quantities and can be frozen in convenient amounts.*

1 pound fresh mushrooms
2 large shallots

2 tablespoons margarine
Vegetable seasoning and
white pepper

Chop the mushrooms and shallots in the food processor. Squeeze the mixture dry in a towel.

Heat the margarine in a skillet. Add mixture and stir over high heat until the mushrooms separate and start to brown. Cook until almost dry. Season with salt and pepper.

.　　.　　.

WHOLE-WHEAT CREPES

*Crepes are the basis of many party dishes. This recipe makes 12 to
14 six-inch crepes or 16 to 18 five-inch crepes. Crepes may be made in an
ordinary skillet, but it is much more fun to make them in a crepe pan, which
can be purchased in any cookware shop. Heat the pan well and brush lightly with
vegetable oil. It is not necessary to oil the pan again. Cooked crepes can
be stacked and frozen for future use. It is very helpful to have a stock in
the freezer. For easier handling, place rounds of wax paper between the crepes.*

¾ cup whole-wheat pastry
　flour
1½ teaspoons baking powder
¼ teaspoon salt substitute
　(optional)

⅛ teaspoon white pepper
2 eggs or egg substitutes
1 cup skim milk
1½ tablespoons sesame oil

Combine the pastry flour, baking powder, and seasonings. In another bowl, beat the eggs until frothy. Add the milk. Stir in the dry ingredients just until blended. Let stand 5 minutes.

Prepare the crepe pan as directed above. Pour in 1½ tablespoons of batter, tilting the pan so that the batter covers the entire bottom in a thin layer. Cook 40 to 50 seconds, or until the surface is covered with little bubbles. Turn the crepe

with a spatula. Cook for 20 to 30 seconds on the second side. If using a skillet, pour in the same amount of batter and spread it gently into a thin circle 5 to 6 inches in diameter.

Crepes can be cooked in advance and reheated just before serving in a 350° oven or in a microwave. Specific directions for individual preparations will be given with the recipes.

.　　.　　.

SOUFFLÉ PANCAKES

Soufflé pancakes are the basis for both savory and sweet dishes.
They also make a pleasant bread accompaniment to a meat or vegetable dish.
Stack the cooked pancakes in a warm oven and serve them whole or
halved with just margarine or with pure maple syrup.

½ cup whole-wheat pastry
    flour
¼ cup unbleached all-purpose
    flour
1 teaspoon baking powder
⅛ teaspoon white pepper

2 eggs, separated (room
    temperature)
1 cup buttermilk
1½ tablespoons oil (safflower or
    peanut)
    Polyunsaturated margarine
    Maple syrup (optional)

Blend the flours, baking powder, and pepper in a mixing bowl. Beat the egg yolks until light. Stir them with the buttermilk and oil into the dry ingredients just until blended. Cover and let stand for 1 hour. Just before cooking beat the egg whites and fold them into the batter.

Heat a nonstick 6-inch skillet. Brush very lightly with corn oil. This is all the grease you will need. Pour a small ladleful of batter into the pan. Cook until the pancake rises and holes appear on the surface. Turn and cook on the other side for 1 minute or less. Remove from the skillet to a platter. Keep the pancakes warm in a 200° oven after they are cooked.

• • •

LO-CHOL PASTRY

Yield: eight 3-inch tart shells, one 2-crust 8-inch pie, or 6-8 small pizza shells

⅔ cup unbleached all-purpose flour
⅔ cup whole-wheat pastry flour
½ teaspoon salt substitute

½ teaspoon sugar
⅓ cup peanut oil
3 teaspoons lemon juice
3½ tablespoons cold water

Place the flour, pastry flour, salt substitute, and sugar in the working bowl of a food processor. Add the oil and lemon juice and spin 2 seconds. Add the water. Spin just until the dough starts to form a ball. Remove from the bowl and knead it lightly into a ball.

Place in plastic wrap and chill 60 minutes. Place the ball on a lightly floured piece of wax paper. Flatten into a disk and sprinkle the top with a little flour. Cover with another piece of wax paper and roll out to the thickness specified in the recipe.

•   •   •

HONEY CHEESE CREAM

Yield: 4-6 servings

1 cup low-fat cottage cheese
1 cup yogurt

⅓ cup honey
1 teaspoon lemon juice

Put the ingredients in a food processor and process until blended. The honey should be at room temperature, the other ingredients very cold. Serve cold, to contrast with a warm pudding. If

made in advance, store in the refrigerator and give the sauce a quick spin before serving so the honey will be well blended with the other ingredients.

•   •   •

WHIPPED DESSERT TOPPING

½ cup water
1 tablespoon lemon juice

2 packets artificial sweetener
½ teaspoon vanilla

Combine all ingredients in a small bowl. Chill in the refrigerator until very cold,

then whip with an electric beater. Use as you would use whipped cream.

•   •   •

14

THREE-GRAIN REFRIGERATOR BREAD OR ROLLS

¾ cup diced potato
½ teaspoon salt
½ teaspoon vegetable seasoning
   or salt substitute
1 cup cold water
1 stick unsalted polyunsaturated
   margarine
¼ cup honey

½ cup skim-milk powder
3 eggs or egg substitutes
2 packages powdered yeast
4 tablespoons lukewarm water
1 teaspoon sugar
2 cups whole-wheat flour
1 cup amaranth flour
2 cups all-purpose unbleached flour

Put the potato, salt, salt substitute, and cold water into a pan. Bring to a boil and cook until the potato is tender. Mash by hand or with an electric beater and add the margarine, honey, and milk powder. Add the eggs one by one, beating after each addition.

Dissolve the yeast and sugar in the lukewarm water and let stand 2 to 3 minutes. Add the lukewarm potato mixture and stir in the flours to make a soft dough. Knead for 10 minutes with the dough hook. Let rise until doubled in volume (1½ hours). Knead down and store overnight in the refrigerator. Take out the required amount and let rise at room temperature until doubled again. Shape into long loaves or individual rolls. Cover and let rise until doubled.

Bake bread in a preheated 425° oven for 10 minutes. Reduce heat to 350° and bake 30 minutes longer.

Bake rolls for 15 to 20 minutes at 400°.

MULTI-GRAIN FOOD PROCESSOR BREAD
Yield: 1 loaf

Making bread in a food processor is very easy, even for someone who has never made bread. If you make the multi-grain variety you will soon earn the price of the machine, given the high prices asked for these healthful natural breads in the market. Experiment with combinations of grains. The loaf will be very compact. Sliced and toasted, it will make a delicious and healthful breakfast.

1½ packages dry yeast
1 teaspoon sugar
1 cup very warm water (115°)
4 tablespoons polyunsaturated, unsalted margarine
1½ cups unbleached all-purpose flour

1 teaspoon salt or salt substitute (optional)
1¼ cups oat bran
¼ cup triticale flour (available at natural food stores)
1 teaspoon peanut or sesame oil

Stir the yeast and sugar into half the warm water. Heat the margarine in the remaining water until it melts. Cool to lukewarm.

Put the all-purpose flour in the food processor bowl. Add the salt and the yeast mixture. Process 1 second. Pour in the margarine mixture through the tube. Process 10 seconds. Add the oat bran and triticale flour and process until it forms a ball (30 to 40 seconds). Do not overprocess.

Lightly oil a 6-cup bowl. Shape the dough into a ball and turn it around in the oiled bowl. Cover with a damp towel and let rise until the dough comes to the top of the bowl. Punch down and form into the shape of a loaf. Place in a lightly oiled bread tin. Cover with a towel and let rise until tripled in volume. Bake in a preheated 375° oven for 45 to 50 minutes. Ten minutes before the end of the baking time brush the top of the loaf with oil. When baked, turn the bread onto a rack to cool.

•　　•　　•

SPRING MENUS

1

Luncheon for Eight

Presentation Salad
Whole-Wheat Popovers
Iced Oranges

·   ·   ·

2

Dinner for Four

Stuffed Fillets of Sole
Steamed Potatoes
Savory Carrots
Danish Strawberry Jell

·   ·   ·

3

Supper for Four to Six

Turkey Pot Roast with Root Vegetables
Salad Rose
Melon Bowls

·   ·   ·

4

Dinner for Four

Basque Chicken
Mother-of-Pearl Rice
Chinese Green Beans
Fresh Pineapple in Honey

·   ·   ·

5

Dinner for Four

Sole in Walnut Sauce
Parmesan Asparagus
Scalloped Tomato Ramekins
Banana Kiwi Coupe

.   .   .

6

Dinner Party for Six

Eggplant Appetizer
Whole-Wheat Bagel Crisps
Baked Trout with Herbs
Saute' of Zucchini and Fresh Spinach
Blueberry Souffle' Pancakes

.   .   .

7

Saturday Supper for Eight

Parslied High-Lysine Cornmeal Souffle'
Asparagus Aspic
Fruit Spiral

.   .   .

Luncheon for Eight

PRESENTATION SALAD
Yield: Serves 8

*This salad makes a beautiful centerpiece.
Once tossed, it makes a delicious main dish or vegetable course.*

½ head best iceberg lettuce (as
    green as possible)
1 small head chicory
½ medium head romaine
1 bunch watercress
6 stalks celery heart
2 hard-cooked eggs plus
    whites of 2 more hard-
    cooked eggs (optional)
1 cup diced cooked turkey or
    chicken
3 tablespoons chopped
    scallions
2 ounces Roquefort or good
    blue cheese

3 tomatoes
1 can anchovy fillets
1 jar roasted peppers
1 large avocado

Dressing:
⅓ cup tarragon vinegar
⅓ cup peanut oil
⅓ cup olive oil
    Teaspoon chopped herbs
    (optional)
    Salt substitute (optional)
    and pepper

Wash the lettuces and spin dry. Pull off the leaves and tender stems of the watercress. Wash and dry. Wrap the lettuces and the watercress separately and pack in plastic bags. Mince the celery and scallions and put in separate bowls. Dice eggs, chicken, and roasted peppers and put in separate bowls. Finely dice the salad greens. Mince the watercress leaves. Dip the tomatoes in boiling water for a few seconds. Peel off the skins. Cut the tomatoes in half and gently squeeze out the seeds and juice. Dice the flesh.

Prepare the dressing: Combine ingredients. Put in a jar and refrigerate.

Peel, halve, seed, and dice the avocado. Place in a sieve. Rinse in cold water and drain. (This will prevent darkening.) Place in a bowl. Spoon a little prepared dressing over the avocado bits.

The salad can be prepared to this point in advance. Cover all the bowls with plastic wrap and refrigerate.

Shortly before lunch: Put a third of the dressing on half the diced salad greens and spread them evenly in the base of a large glass salad bowl. Arrange the celery, the diced eggs, the chicken, the scallions, the cheese, the roasted peppers, the remaining salad greens, diced tomatoes and avocado bits in parallel strips, alternating the colors. Surround the edge with the watercress leaves and decorate the egg strips with anchovy fillets. Bring to the table with the rest of the dressing in a cruet. Toss at the table after everyone has seen your creation.

Hard-cooked eggs add both taste and texture to this salad, but you may leave them out if you wish—the salad will be good without them.

•   •   •

WHOLE-WHEAT POPOVERS
Yield: 8 popovers

All ingredients should be at room temperature.

⅔ cup whole-wheat pastry
    flour
⅓ cup all-purpose unbleached
    flour

1 cup skim milk
2 eggs or egg substitutes

Preheat the oven to 450°. Vegetable-spray eight 7-ounce muffin tins or Pyrex custard cups. Stir the flours and milk until blended. Beat in the eggs one by one, beating just until you have a batter the consistency of thick cream. Fill the prepared cups ⅓ full and place in the oven. At the end of 15 minutes, reduce the heat to 350° and cook 20 to 25 minutes longer. If the popovers have to wait, pierce them with a skewer to let the steam escape. They will stand for several minutes but are always best eaten as soon as they are baked.

• • •

ICED ORANGES
Yield: 8 servings

8 eating oranges (navel, Jaffa,
    Clementine)
2 juice oranges
1 teaspoon lemon juice

1 packet sugar substitute
    (optional)
    Shredded coconut or
    almonds

Peel the eating oranges and remove every bit of white fiber possible. Slice the oranges quite thin into a shallow dessert bowl so as to catch all possible juices. Squeeze the juice oranges and combine with the lemon juice. Add the sugar substitute if desired. Cover the bowl and chill for at least 3 hours. Just before serving sprinkle with either shredded coconut or almonds.

• • •

Dinner for Four

STUFFED FILLETS OF SOLE
Yield: Serves 4

8 sole fillets (3 to 3½ ounces
    each)
4 medium large shrimp
½ pound fresh broccoli
2 cups Chicken Broth
    (page 5)
2 tablespoons
    polyunsaturated unsalted
    margarine
    Salt substitute or vegetable
    seasonings (optional)
    White pepper
⅛ teaspoon cornstarch
1 large shallot, chopped fine
¾ cup Cornstarch Milk
    (page 6)

4 peppercorns
2 teaspoons lemon juice
½ teaspoon dried tarragon
    Pimiento
    Watercress or Italian
    parsley

Court Bouillon:
2 cups water plus ½ cup
    bottled clam broth or 2½
    cups fish stock
2 slices of onion
    Pinch thyme
1 bay leaf
2 strips lemon peel

This recipe was designed for Dover sole, which is a more accommodating shape than the American sole. Nevertheless, it can be done. Choose fillets of approximately the same length (approximately 4 to 4½ inches). If some are too wide, cut them in half lengthwise. Place two fillets between sheets of wax paper, one overlapping the other lengthwise by an inch so that you have a long piece of fish. Pound with a cleaver or other flat instrument until they are ¼-inch thick and well stuck together. Carefully transfer the fish to a working surface. Repeat the process until you have 4 long pieces of fish.

Bring the bouillon ingredients and any fish trimmings to a simmer in a large shallow saucepan or skillet. Cover and simmer 10 minutes.

Peel and clean the raw shrimp. Keep in refrigerator.

Trim the broccoli, using only the flowerets and tender stems. Bring the chicken broth to a boil and add the broccoli. Cook until just tender, about 5 minutes. Drain and save the broth. Process the broccoli in a food processor with 1 tablespoon margarine.

Blend the cornstarch into ¼ cup cold water. Heat ½ cup of the chicken broth in a small saucepan. (Save the rest for sipping. It's delicious.) Add the cornstarch and cook until thickened. Add to the broccoli. Season to taste. Cool to lukewarm.

Spread each fish strip with a quarter of the broccoli mixture. Roll up like a jelly roll. Fasten with a toothpick. Place the rolls in a pan just large enough to accommodate the rolls in a single layer. Place a shrimp on the upper side of each roll in the center. Pour in the white wine. It should come halfway up the sides of the rolls. Cover with foil and bake 15 to 20 minutes at 375°.

Transfer the fish to a baking sheet. Cover and keep warm. Quickly boil down the liquid to measure 1 cup. Sauté the chopped shallot in 1 tablespoon of margarine in a small skillet just until tender. Add the reserved cooking liquid, the cornstarch milk, the lemon juice, and the tarragon. Simmer the sauce until it is slightly thickened.

Pour the sauce in the bottom of a heated shallow platter. Place the fillets on top of the sauce and garnish each one with pimiento and a little watercress or parsley.

. . .

STEAMED POTATOES
Yield: 4 servings

1 pound medium-size potatoes

Wash and peel the potatoes. Place in the upper part of a steamer or, lacking that, place in a colander. Cook covered over rapidly boiling water for 15 to 20 minutes or until tender. Serve whole or force through a ricer or food mill.

. . .

"Well, we're looking at two coats of icing, definitely have to reglaze those windows, and I'm afraid total gumdrop replacement...."

SAVORY CARROTS

Yield: 4 servings

*The carrots and sauce can both be prepared in advance
and tossed together over medium heat just before serving.*

3 cups small peeled California
   carrots (available at
   supermarket)
2 tablespoons polyun-
   saturated margarine
1 clove garlic, pressed

½ teaspoon fresh summer
   savory
⅓ cup chopped chives
   Salt substitute or vegetable
   seasoning (optional)
   White pepper

Place the small carrots in cold water. Bring them to a boil and cook 12 to 14 minutes or just until tender. Drain thoroughly.

Heat the margarine with the garlic, savory, and chives over low heat for 2 minutes. Add the carrots and toss them until well coated and very hot. Season as desired. Use quite a lot of pepper for a very good flavor. Transfer to a heated vegetable dish.

•   •   •

DANISH STRAWBERRY JELL

Yield: 4 servings

2 cups water
1½ pints strawberries, washed
   and hulled
2 tablespoons sugar
3 tablespoons potato flour

3 tablespoons water
   Whipped Dessert Topping
   (page 14)
4 small strawberries for
   garnish

Bring the 2 cups of water to a boil. Add the berries and sugar and simmer 2 minutes. Mix the potato flour with the 3 tablespoons water. Add to the berries. Stir until the mixture boils. Pour into dessert glasses. Cool and then chill.

To serve: Top each serving with a spoonful of whipped topping and garnish with a small strawberry.

•   •   •

3

Supper for Four to Six

TURKEY POT ROAST WITH ROOT VEGETABLES

Yield: 4-6 servings

2 turkey thighs, boned
 (approximately 2 pounds)
2 cups chicken or turkey
 broth (unsalted)
½ cup chopped onion
¼ cup shredded carrots
2 cloves garlic, pressed
½ cup chopped celery
2 tablespoons chopped
 parsley

¼ teaspoon freshly ground
 black pepper
½ teaspoon vegetable
 seasoning or salt
 substitute (optional)
½ bay leaf
½ teaspoon powdered thyme
4-6 medium-size potatoes
8-12 medium-size carrots
8-12 medium-size white turnips

Remove the skin and thereby almost all of the fat from the thighs. Vegetable-spray a non-stick deep pan. Heat it well and sear the thighs on both sides briefly. Add the fat-free broth, onion, carrots, garlic, celery, and the seasonings. Bring to a boil on top of the stove and then bake covered 1 hour and 15 minutes in a 350° oven.

Prepare the potatoes, carrots, and white turnips, and cook them separately in boiling water, starting each one in cold water so that they will be cooked when the pot roast is ready. The carrots and potatoes will take about 20 minutes; the turnips about 15 minutes.

Remove the thighs from the pan to a cutting board. Cut into thin slices on the diagonal. Remove the bay leaf from the sauce and taste for seasoning. The sauce will be thickened by the vegetables. If it is too thin, boil down quickly for a few minutes. Pour the sauce into a preheated deep platter. Lay the slices in the sauce and surround decoratively with the cooked potatoes, carrots, and turnips. Sprinkle with the chopped parsley.

• • •

"Could I have the comic section?"

SALAD ROSE
Yield: 4 servings

*This is another salad that serves as a centerpiece until it is tossed
at the table. Make sure that the greens are washed separately and carefully
dried. Keep in the refrigerator until just before mealtime and serve
the dressing in a cruet. Toss just before serving.*

1 small head garden lettuce
1 small head red lettuce
1 small head curly green lettuce

¼ pound spinach leaves
1 tomato
Italian Dressing (page 8)

Wash the greens and dry them well. Cut the tomato in sections and place it like an almost closed bud in the center of the bowl. Starting with the dark spinach leaves make concentric circles around the tomato of the greens going from darkest to the very lightest. Cover and refrigerate.

Prepare the Italian Dressing and put it in a cruet or jar. Shake well before adding to the salad and tossing. Serve on separate plates.

•　•　•

MELON BOWLS
Yield: 4 servings

2 ripe cantaloupes
1 bunch small green seedless
   grapes
1 ripe banana

1 teaspoon lemon juice
1 packet artificial sweetener
   (optional)
Grape leaves

Halve the cantaloupes and scoop out in small balls using a melon scooper. Stem the grapes and mix them with the cantaloupe balls. Dice the banana in small dice. Add them and the lemon juice to the mixture. If desired, add the sweetener. Cover and chill.

Cut a thin slice from the bottom of each cantaloupe half so it will sit on a plate without tipping. Scrape out any orange flesh. Turn them upside down to drain in the refrigerator in a shallow dish.

To serve: Line each of four individual plates with a large grape leaf. Place a cantaloupe half on the leaf and fill with the fruit mixture.

•　•　•

26

Dinner for Four

BASQUE CHICKEN
Yield: 4 servings

3½ pounds chicken, quartered
2 medium tomatoes
1 medium-size onion
2 cloves garlic
1 pound green peppers
2 tablespoons olive oil
2 tablespoons polyun-
   saturated margarine
⅔ cup water

1 tablespoon lemon juice
4 sprigs parsley
1 imported bay leaf
3 sprigs thyme or ½ teaspoon
   dried thyme
Salt substitute (optional) or
   vegetable seasoning
Freshly ground black pepper
1 tablespoon chopped parsley

Remove all skin from the chicken. Wash the chicken and pat dry. Peel, halve, seed, and dice the tomatoes. Peel and chop the onion very fine. Crush, peel, and chop the garlic fine. Wash the peppers. Halve them and remove the seeds and ribs. Chop fine. Heat the oil and margarine in a large skillet, large enough to accommodate the chicken in one layer. Brown the chicken quarters well on both sides, turning the pieces over with tongs. When well browned, transfer them to a platter. Reduce the heat a little and add the garlic, onions, and peppers. Stir until the onions are golden and put back the chicken. Add the tomatoes, water, lemon juice, and the parsley, bay leaf, and thyme tied in a little bundle. Season with pepper and salt substitute and simmer gently for 30 minutes or until the chicken is cooked.

To serve: Using tongs, place the chicken pieces in a shallow serving platter. Keep warm. If the sauce is too liquid, boil it down rapidly to a thicker consistency. Pour the sauce over the chicken. Sprinkle with chopped parsley.

• • •

*Bill dropped the cheese and for a second
everyone froze. . . .*

MOTHER-OF-PEARL RICE
Yield: 4 servings

4 tablespoons polyun-
saturated margarine
1 medium onion, chopped fine
1 cup unpolished long-grain
rice

2 cups unsalted chicken broth
or hot water
Salt substitute or vege-
table seasoning (optional)
¼ teaspoon white pepper

Heat 2 tablespoons of margarine in a skillet. Sauté the onion over low heat until well coated with margarine. Add the rice and continue to cook gently until the rice is translucent (in France, this is called "mother pearling"). Add the liquid and cover tightly. Cook over moderate heat for 17 minutes. Remove from the heat but keep covered for several minutes to continue the cooking. Fluff the rice with two forks, adding the remaining margarine and seasonings as desired. Serve in a heated vegetable dish.

• • •

CHINESE GREEN BEANS
Yield: 4 servings

1 pound fresh green beans
¼ cup unsalted roasted
peanuts

2 tablespoons oyster sauce
(available in Oriental
grocery stores)
⅓ cup rice vinegar
1 clove garlic, pressed

Wash and trim the beans, cutting them in thirds unless they are very small. Boil or steam the beans until just tender. Meanwhile, crush the peanuts in a food processor or with a hand chopper. Place in a warm serving bowl and stir in the oyster sauce and the vinegar. Press the garlic into the mixture and mix. Drain the beans thoroughly and put them in the bowl. Toss well before serving. Serve at room temperature.

• • •

FRESH PINEAPPLE IN HONEY
Yield: 4 servings

1 medium-size fresh, ripe
pineapple

⅓ cup honey
2 teaspoons lemon juice

Peel the pineapple. Remove the core and cut the ripe flesh into bite-size pieces. Place in a non-metal bowl. Warm the honey over low heat. Remove from the stove, add the lemon juice and stir until blended. Pour over the pineapple and chill in the refrigerator. Serve in individual dessert dishes.

• • •

Dinner for Four

SOLE IN WALNUT SAUCE
Yield: 4 servings

4 fillets of sole (5 to 6 ounces each)
Whole-wheat pastry flour
⅛ teaspoon white pepper
4 tablespoons polyun-saturated margarine

1 tablespoon peanut oil
4 tablespoons coarsely chopped walnuts
Juice of ½ lemon
2 tablespoons finely chopped parsley

Dip the fillets of sole lightly in the pastry flour mixed with the pepper. Shake off any excess flour.

Heat 2 tablespoons of the margarine and the peanut oil in a skillet. When very hot, sauté the fish for 90 seconds on each side. Do not overcook. Transfer the fish to a heated platter. Pour off the fat from the pan and wipe it out quickly with a paper towel. Heat the remaining margarine. Add the walnuts and toss until lightly browned. Add the lemon juice and the parsley and pour over the fish. Serve on heated plates.

• • •

PARMESAN ASPARAGUS
Yield: 4 servings

2 pounds freshly picked asparagus
4 slices whole-wheat bread

3 tablespoons poly-unsaturated margarine, melted
White pepper
Parmesan cheese

Wash and trim the asparagus. If it is not freshly picked, peeling the stems will enhance the flavor. Place the asparagus in a skillet of cold water. Bring to a boil over moderately high heat and cook just until tender. The time will vary according to the thickness of the stems. Do not overcook.

Meanwhile, toast the bread lightly and heat the margarine until it bubbles. Place the toast on individual salad plates. Using tongs lift the asparagus by quarter lots from the skillet, shaking off the excess water. Place on the toast. Sprinkle with white pepper, hot margarine, and finally with the Parmesan cheese. Serve immediately.

• • •

SCALLOPED TOMATO RAMEKINS

Yield: 4 servings

2 slices homemade whole-
    wheat bread
2 tablespoons grated onion
1 can (16 ounces) Italian
    peeled tomatoes
    Artificial sweetener

⅛ teaspoon freshly ground
    black pepper
¼ teaspoon dried basil
    Vegetable seasoning or salt
    substitute
2 teaspoons polyunsaturated
    margarine

Cut the bread into large dice to make the croutons, removing the crusts or not as you prefer. Toast them lightly under the broiler.

Drain the juice from the tomatoes and bring it to a boil with the onion. Remove from the heat and stir in ¼ teaspoon of the sweetener. Lightly oil 4 ramekins or Pyrex custard dishes. Scatter half the croutons on the bottoms of the ramekins. Divide the tomatoes among the ramekins and sprinkle with the pepper, basil, and vegetable seasoning. Divide the juice between the ramekins.

Heat the margarine in a small skillet and toss the remaining croutons. Sprinkle over the tomatoes. Bake 20 minutes at 350°.

•   •   •

BANANA KIWI COUPÉ

Yield: 4 servings

Prepare this just before serving.
Use only ripe fruit because they are so much sweeter.

3 ripe bananas

4 ripe kiwis

Peel the bananas and cut them into ½-inch slices. Peel the kiwis and cut into wedges. Combine, toss them quickly, and serve in individual sherbet glasses.

30

Dinner Party for Six

EGGPLANT APPETIZER
Yield: 6 servings

3 medium-size eggplants
1 clove garlic
1 small onion

1-2 teaspoons lemon or lime
    juice (according to taste)
2-3 tablespoons olive oil
2 tablespoons chopped parsley

Wash and dry the eggplant. Grill over high heat or under a preheated broiler for 20 minutes, turning frequently until charred all over the outside.

Split open lengthwise and drain in a colander for 15 minutes.

Crush the garlic and puree with the onion in a food processor. Spoon the eggplant out of the skin into the feed tube and purée. Season with lemon or lime juice and add oil very gradually, only enough to make the mixture shiny. Stir in parsley and serve in small bowls with Whole-Wheat Bagel Crisps.

• • •

WHOLE-WHEAT BAGEL CRISPS
Yield: 6 bagels

6 fresh whole-wheat bakery
    bagels

1-2 tablespoons olive oil
    (optional)

Freeze the fresh bagels for 20 minutes in the deep freeze. Cut them in half vertically and slice them horizontally ⅛-inch thick by hand, or easier still, in the food processor. Line a baking sheet with aluminum foil and preheat the pan in a 400° oven. For richer flavor, paint the

foil lightly with olive oil. Place the bagel slices on the foil, brush lightly with the oil if desired and toast under the broiler until browned. Keep a careful eye on the slices so that they do not burn. Turn once and brown quickly.

• • •

BAKED TROUT WITH HERBS

Yield: 6 servings

Trout farms are appearing across the nation and are the source of much gastronomical pleasure. Order the trout in advance and inform the owner of the exact time you want to pick them up, so that he will kill and clean the fish at the last possible moment. The fresher the fish, the more delicious the result.

6 very fresh trout
4 tablespoons Italian parsley,
   chopped
4 tablespoons chopped chives
2 tablespoons dried tarragon
   or vegetable seasoning

Freshly ground pepper
¼ cup melted polyunsaturated
   margarine
3 teaspoons lemon juice

Leave the trout whole if possible, with the head and tail on. Wash and pat dry with toweling.

Combine the chopped parsley, chives, and tarragon or vegetable seasoning.

Combine the margarine and lemon juice.

Make 3 or 4 diagonal slits on the top side of each fish. Spread the slits apart with your fingers and insert the mixture of herbs. Place the fish in a shallow, lightly oiled baking pan. Sprinkle with the pepper. Pour the melted margarine and lemon juice sauce over the trout, allowing 2½ teaspoons to each trout. Bake 20 to 25 minutes at 400°, basting every 5 minutes.

•   •   •

SAUTÉ OF ZUCCHINI AND FRESH SPINACH
Yield: 6 servings

1½ pounds zucchini
1½ pounds fresh spinach
2 tablespoons olive oil
2 tablespoons polyunsaturated
   margarine

1 medium-size onion, sliced
   Vegetable seasoning or salt
   substitute (optional)
Pepper

Trim the zucchini and wash well. Cut into large dice and place in a colander. Let drain, pressing gently with your fingers, while preparing the spinach.

Wash the spinach well and remove all but the very tender stems and leaves.

Heat 1 tablespoon of oil and 1 table-spoon of margarine in a wok or saucepan. When the margarine is melted add the spinach. Toss and cook for 5 minutes.

Heat the remaining oil and margarine in the wok and add the sliced onion. Toss and cook for 1 minute. Add the zucchini.

Toss and cook for 2 to 3 minutes or until tender. Press out any liquid from the spinach and add the spinach to the zucchini. Toss until thoroughly heated.

Season as desired and serve in a heated vegetable dish.

. . .

BLUEBERRY SOUFFLÉ PANCAKES
Yield: 6 servings

   Soufflé Pancakes (page 13)
1 pint fresh blueberries
2 packets artificial sweetener
   (optional)

⅛ teaspoon nutmeg
   Honey Cheese Cream
   (page 14)

Prepare and make the soufflé pancakes. Keep warm in a low-temperature oven.

Toss the blueberries with 2 packets of the artificial sweetener and the nutmeg. Save out a third for garnish.

Prepare the Honey Cheese Cream.

To serve: Put a large spoonful of blueberries in each pancake. Fold over and top with the Honey Cheese Cream. Serve on individual dessert plates garnished with a few blueberries.

. . .

7

Saturday Supper for Eight

PARSLIED HIGH-LYSINE CORNMEAL SOUFFLÉ
Yield: 8 servings

2 cups low-fat milk
2 cups defatted Chicken
    Broth (page 5)
⅔ cup high-lysine cornmeal
2 tablespoons polyunsaturated
    margarine
6 tablespoons grated
    Parmesan or Romano cheese

4 egg yolks, beaten
6 egg whites, beaten stiff
    Salt substitute or vegetable
    seasoning (optional)
¼ teaspoon white pepper
2 tablespoons chopped parsley

Heat the milk and chicken broth to the boiling point. Stir in the cornmeal and the margarine. Reduce the heat and stir in the grated cheese. Cook to a thick mush, stirring frequently. Add the beaten egg yolks and stir 1 minute longer. Season to taste. Cool.

Before baking, stir in the parsley and ¼ of the egg whites until well blended. This will lighten the mixture. Fold in the remaining egg whites. Transfer to a well-oiled baking dish. Bake 45 minutes at 350°. Serve hot.

• • • •

ASPARAGUS ASPIC
Yield: 8 servings

3 packages plain gelatin
1½ cups water
1¼ cups chicken broth
3 tablespoons lemon juice
¾ teaspoon salt
   substitute (optional)
¼ cup chopped pimientos
2 pounds asparagus
½ cup chopped green onions
1 cup chopped celery

Dressing:
1 cup farmer's cheese
½ cup light (reduced-calorie)
   mayonnaise
2 tablespoons lemon juice
2 tablespoons Dijon mustard
¼ teaspoon paprika
⅛ teaspoon white pepper
1 tablespoon chopped chives

Lightly coat a large (2 qt.) ring mold with vegetable spray.

Cut the asparagus tips and tender parts of the stems of half the asparagus in ½-inch pieces. Boil in a pan of water for 4 or 5 minutes or until tender but still crisp. Drain. Rinse in cold water and drain again. At the same time, cut the top 4 inches off the remaining asparagus and cook in water 8 to 10 minutes or until tender. Drain. Rinse in cold water. Drain again. Let cool. Set aside for garnish.

Soften the gelatin in ½ cup of the water. Combine 1 cup of water, the chicken broth, the lemon juice, and the salt substitute, if desired, in a saucepan and bring to a boil. Remove from the heat and stir in the gelatin. Pour into a metal bowl and place the bowl in a pan of ice. Stir frequently until slightly syrupy and cool to the touch. Remove from the ice.

Meanwhile, dice the peppers, the celery, and the onions. Stir the vegetables, including the asparagus pieces, into the aspic and pour the mixture into the mold. Chill several hours in the refrigerator. Turn onto a salad platter. Fill the center with the dressing and garnish with the asparagus tips.

The dressing: Whisk all the ingredients except the chives in a bowl. Chill until serving time. Garnish with the chopped chives.

•   •   •

FRUIT SPIRAL

Yield: 8 servings

It is important to pick the fruit carefully because sweetness lies in ripe fruit.

2 navel oranges
1 grapefruit
1 cantaloupe
2 red Delicious apples
2 very ripe kiwis

2 ripe bananas
1 pint ripe strawberries
　Juice of 1 lemon
2 packets artificial sweetener

Peel the oranges and grapefruit. Divide into sections, removing all possible white fiber. Halve and peel the cantaloupe and cut into long thin sections. Wash and halve the apples. Cut into thin sections leaving the peel on but cutting out the core. Place in a small bowl and sprinkle with a little of the lemon juice.

Save out the most beautiful strawberry and quarter the rest. Put the large strawberry in the center of a shallow dessert platter. Arrange the fruit spiral-like around the strawberry, with a secondary spiral nearer the edge of the platter. Use the colors of the fruit as your guide. Slice the peeled kiwis and bananas and place them alternately around the edge. Combine the juice with the sweetener and sprinkle it over the fruit. Serve very cold.

• • •

SUMMER MENUS

1

Luncheon for Eight

Nicoise Salad
Oat Bran Banana Muffins
Watermelon Balls in Pink Lemonade

• • •

2

Dinner Party for Four

Jellied Tarragon Chicken Consommé
Do-It-Ahead Normandy Sole
New Potatoes Boiled in Their Jackets
Carrots and Snow Peas
Citrus Apricot Cup

• • •

3

Dinner for Six

Deviled Rock Cornish Game Hens
Basmati Rice Salad
Curried Zucchini
Cold Mango Pureé

• • •

4

Dinner Party for Six

Leeks Vinaigrette
Souffléed Swordfish
Broiled Tomatoes
Broccoli with Pesto
Gratin of Mixed Fruit

· · ·

5

Dinner Party for Eight

Chilled Cucumber Tarragon Soup
Charcoaled Chicken
All-Year-Round Corn
Green Bean Salad
Fresh Strawberry Compote

· · ·

Luncheon for Eight

NICOISE SALAD
Yield: 8 servings

*There are almost as many versions of this salad in southern France as
there are housewives. It can be very complicated or as simple as you want to make it.
It's easy to decorate and makes a wonderful luncheon.*

Vinaigrette:
⅓ cup red wine vinegar
1 teaspoon Dijon mustard
½ teaspoon salt substitute or
vegetable seasoning
¼ teaspoon freshly ground
black pepper
⅛ cup sesame oil
⅛ cup olive oil
Salad:
1 head garden lettuce
2 pounds medium-size
redskin potatoes
2-3 cloves garlic
½ cup chopped green onions

2 cans (6¾ ounces) water-
packed tuna
1 teaspoon salt substitute or
vegetable seasoning
1 pound fresh green beans
1 long seedless cucumber
½ cup sliced radishes
½ pint cherry tomatoes
2 tablespoons drained capers
(optional)
8 anchovy fillets
8 imported black olives
½ cup (reduced calorie)
mayonnaise
Italian parsley

Prepare the vinaigrette. Combine the ingredients in a covered jar so that it is easy to shake.

Wash the lettuce and divide it into loose leaves. Chill until just before you make the salad.

Choose potatoes of nearly equal size so that they can all be cooked to tender at the same time. Scrub but do not peel. Put the potatoes in a pan of cold water and bring to a boil. Boil until tender (20 to 25 minutes).

Meanwhile, chop the garlic very fine and chop the green onions.

Drain the tuna and flake it coarsely.

Wash the beans. Clip off the ends and cut into inch-long pieces. Boil or steam them for 10 to 12 minutes. When tender-crisp, drain them and freshen them under running cold water.

Drain the potatoes and place in a wooden bowl. Let them cool for 5 minutes.

Chop the potatoes coarsely and season with ¼ cup of well-shaken vinaigrette. Combine with the tuna, green onions, garlic, and 1 teaspoon of vegetable seasoning or salt substitute. Mix carefully to avoid crushing the potatoes. Cool completely.

Toss the beans in 4 tablespoons of vinaigrette and the seasonings.

To assemble the salad: Prepare the garnish: Scrub and slice the cucumber very thin. Prepare the radishes and tomatoes. Rinse the excess salt out of the anchovy fillets and pit the black olives.

Stack several lettuce leaves on top of one another. Roll into a tight roll and using a large knife, cut the roll into thin slices to shred it. Continue until all the lettuce is shredded. Line a large platter with lettuce, saving enough to go around the outside edge.

Mound the salad down the center of the platter. Surround it with a ring of green beans and then a ring of shredded lettuce. Spoon the rest of the vinaigrette over the salad and grind black pepper over the top. Garnish decoratively with the sliced cucumber, sliced radishes, tomato halves, capers, anchovies, black olives, and Italian parsley.

With mayonnaise in a pastry bag or teaspoon, draw lines to indicate the 8 serving portions. Extra mayonnaise can be served in a separate bowl for those who want it.

．　　　．　　　．

OAT BRAN BANANA MUFFINS
Yield: 12 large muffins

1 teaspoon peanut or corn oil
1 cup oat bran
1½ cups unbleached all-purpose flour
1 tablespoon baking powder
½ teaspoon salt
2 tablespoons brown sugar

1 egg or 2 egg whites
½ cup mashed bananas
1 cup low-fat milk
4 tablespoons polyunsaturated salt-free margarine, melted
½ teaspoon almond extract

Preheat the oven to 375°.

Use the peanut or corn oil to oil 12 non-stick muffin tins.

Mix the dry ingredients in one bowl.

Beat the egg or egg whites until frothy in another bowl. Add the bananas, milk, margarine, and extract. Mix well and stir gently into the dry ingredients, stirring only until blended. Do not worry about any small lumps. Let stand 5 minutes.

Fill the muffin tins two-thirds full and bake 20 minutes. These are best piping hot.

．　　　．　　　．

41

WATERMELON BALLS IN PINK LEMONADE

Yield: 8 servings

6 cups watermelon balls
1 can pink lemonade
   concentrate

Mint leaves

Scoop balls from a ripe watermelon. Place in a large covered container. Dilute the lemonade concentrate with half the required water. Pour enough to cover the watermelon balls. Cover and refrigerate for several hours. Serve in individual dishes, each garnished with a mint leaf.

• • •

Dinner Party for Four

JELLIED TARRAGON CHICKEN CONSOMMÉ

Yield: 4 servings

On a hot summer night nothing is more refreshing than a cold clear consommé.

4 cups Chicken Broth
   (page 5)
2 egg whites
⅛ teaspoon salt substitute
   (optional)
⅛ teaspoon white pepper

2 teaspoons lemon juice
   Few drops yellow vegetable
   coloring (optional)
   Branch of tarragon
1 envelope gelatin
4 thin slices lemon

Chicken broth, made at home, usually becomes jellied when cold, but even so, it is usually wise to give it the little extra assurance of extra gelatin. Before adding the gelatin you will need to clarify the stock so that it will be a clear and sparkling consommé.

Put the broth in a large saucepan. Heat it to lukewarm. Remove 8 small tarragon leaves for decoration and break up the rest into the pan of broth.

Beat the egg whites with the small quantities of salt substitute and pepper and the lemon juice just until frothy. Add to the broth and stir gently over medium heat with a wooden spoon just until it starts to boil. Simmer 10 minutes over very low heat.

Line a colander with a damp, clean dish towel and place it over a pan. Carefully pour the broth through the dish towel. It will become a clear consommé. If the color is dull and gray add a few drops of vegetable coloring for eye appeal.

Moisten the gelatin in 2 tablespoons of cold water. Bring the consommé to a full boil and stir in the gelatin. Reduce the heat and stir until the gelatin dissolves. Cool to lukewarm and pour into individual small soup bowls. Chill in the refrigerator and decorate each with a slice of lemon and a tarragon leaf.

. . .

DO-IT-AHEAD NORMANDY SOLE
Yield: 4 servings

Fish:
4 sole fillets (5 to 6 ounces each)

Court Bouillon:
2 cups water plus ½ cup bottled clam broth or 2½ cups fish stock
2 slices of onion
Pinch thyme
1 bay leaf
2 strips lemon peel
4 peppercorns

Garnish:
8 medium-size mushrooms
2 teaspoons polyunsaturated margarine
8 medium large shrimp
Lemon slices
Parsley

Sauce:
1¼ cups reduced stock
1 tablespoon cornstarch
1½ teaspoons lemon juice
2 tablespoons polyunsaturated margarine
½ cup Cornstarch Milk (page 6)
Salt substitute or vegetable seasoning (optional)
White pepper

Trim the fillets so they are of equal size and shape.

Bring the bouillon ingredients and any fish trimmings to a simmer in a large shallow saucepan or skillet. Cover and simmer 10 minutes.

Trim and briefly wash the mushrooms. Separate the caps from the stems. Slice the stems and add to the bouillon. Sauté the caps in a small skillet in the 2 teaspoons of margarine, turning each one once. Set aside.

Add the shrimp to the bouillon and simmer very gently 30 to 60 seconds or just until they turn pink. Remove with a slotted spoon. Remove their shells, throwing the shells back into the bouillon. Simmer covered for 5 minutes. Strain the bouillon into a larger skillet.

Poach the fillets in the bouillon just until opaque. Remove carefully with a slotted spatula to a platter or tray lined with 2 dish towels. DO NOT overcook the fish.

Increase the heat under the skillet and boil down the bouillon until it measures approximately 1¼ cups. Strain into the top part of a double boiler and bring to a boil. Blend the cornstarch with a little cold water. Add to the boiling bouillon and cook over boiling water for 10 minutes. Add the margarine, lemon juice, and cornstarch milk, and whisk well. Season to taste.

The dish can be prepared to this point the morning before serving or even the day before, in which case everything should be covered and stored in the refrigerator.

To serve: Preheat the oven to 300°. Arrange the sole on a large heatproof serving platter. Top with the sauce. Place in the oven and bake for 10 to 15 minutes or until the sauce is bubbly and lightly browned. The garnishes should be reheated but not cooked. Garnish the platter with the mushrooms and shrimp attractively arranged. Sprinkle with chopped parsley and decorate with lemon slices.

•   •   •

NEW POTATOES BOILED IN THEIR JACKETS
Yield: 4 servings

1 pound new potatoes

If possible, choose small red potatoes of approximately the same size for this recipe. Wash them well.

Put in a pan of cold water. Bring to a boil and boil 10 to 12 minutes or until just tender. Drain. Do not season or add butter or margarine because the sauce from the Normandy Sole will suffice.

•   •   •

CARROTS AND SNOW PEAS
Yield: 4 servings

½ **pound snow peas**
2 **large fresh carrots**
2 **tablespoons sesame oil**
1½ **tablespoons polyun-**
    saturated margarine

Salt substitute or vegetable
    seasoning or reduced-sodium
    soy sauce
Freshly ground black pepper

Trim the peas.

Peel the carrots, cut them into 2½-inch lengths and julienne them by hand or in the food processor.

Bring a pan of water to a full boil. Throw in the peas and count to ten. Retrieve the peas with a slotted spoon and transfer them to a bowl of ice water.

Add the julienne carrots to the same pan and when the water returns to a boil, cook for 1 or 2 minutes. Transfer them to another bowl of ice water. Drain both vegetables well. (This can be done in advance.)

Just before serving, heat the margarine and oil in a large skillet or in a wok. Add the vegetables and cook, tossing frequently, for 2 minutes or until heated through. Add pepper and other seasoning as desired and serve in a heated vegetable dish.

•   •   •

CITRUS APRICOT CUP

Yield: 4 servings

1 Temple or Clementine
   orange
1 lemon
½ pound unsulphured apricots

4 tablespoons brown sugar
   (optional)
1 cup plain yogurt
   Mint leaves

Peel the orange and lemon and remove as much of the white fiber as possible. Put the fruit in a saucepan. Add ¼ cup of water. Bring to a boil and simmer tightly covered for 15 minutes. Cool slightly and spin the fruit and cooking liquid in the food processor to make a smooth pureé. Add sugar, if desired. Fold in the yogurt. Serve in individual sherbet glasses garnished with a mint leaf.

.   .   .

3

Dinner for Six

DEVILED ROAST ROCK CORNISH GAME HENS

Yield: Serves 6

6 tablespoons reduced-sodium
   soy sauce
¼ cup honey
2 tablespoons cider vinegar
3 Rock Cornish Hens, split

2 tablespoons sesame oil
3 tablespoons Dijon mustard
   Freshly ground black pepper
   Watercress

Combine the soy sauce, honey, and vinegar in a large shallow bowl. Remove the backbones from the hens and place the hens, skin side down, in the bowl. Let them marinate for 30 minutes.

Preheat the oven to 425°.

Line the rack of a broiling pan with foil. Place the hens on the rack, skin side down. Paint them with the oil and season with black pepper. Roast 15 minutes.

Meanwhile boil down the marinade to half its original quantity. Whisk in the mustard. Turn the hens skin side up. Paint the hens with the marinade and continue basting frequently while the hens roast for another 10 to 15 minutes. The juices should run clear when pricked with a fork.

Transfer the hens to a heated platter. Garnish with watercress.

.   .   .

BASMATI RICE SALAD
Yield: 6 servings

Basmati rice is grown in the foothills of the Himalayas in India and has a delicious flavor. It is available in natural food stores. If it is unavailable, use brown rice and cook 45 minutes.

1 cup Basmati rice
6 firm ripe tomatoes
3 zucchini
½ cup green onions (green and white parts)
2 tablespoons toasted slivered almonds

Dressing:
¼ teaspoon dried oregano
¼ teaspoon dried thyme
⅓ cup fresh basil leaves
⅓ cup red wine vinegar
⅔ cup olive oil
Black pepper

Garnish:
Several large basil leaves
2 anchovy fillets

Soak the rice overnight in water. Add gradually to rapidly boiling water and cook for 25 minutes. The rice should be tender but firm. Drain and rinse in cool water. Drain again.

Prepare vegetables: Peel, seed, and dice the tomatoes into ⅓-inch cubes. If only winter tomatoes are available, substitute well-drained canned, peeled, Italian plum tomatoes for half of them.

Wash the zucchini and cut them into ⅓-inch cubes. Chop the green onions. Toast the slivered almonds. Mix the rice and vegetables in a round bowl.

To make the dressing, place all the ingredients in a blender or food processor and spin until well homogenized. Toss the rice and vegetables with the dressing. Mound on a lettuce-lined round platter and decorate with basil leaves and anchovy fillets. Serve at room temperature.

• • •

"We've got two kids and one in the oven."

46

CURRIED ZUCCHINI

Yield: 6 servings

This can be made in advance and reheated in the microwave or in a saucepan.

5 zucchini (medium size)
¼ cup olive oil
1 cup Chicken Broth (page 5)
1½ teaspoons curry powder
2 tablespoons cornstarch

2 tablespoons water
1 tablespoon cider vinegar
    Salt substitute (optional)
    Freshly ground black pepper

Wash and trim the zucchini. Cut them by hand or in the food processor into ⅛-inch slices. Heat the olive oil in a large skillet. Sauté the zucchini slices for 2 to 3 minutes without letting them brown. Add the broth and the curry. Stir well and cover. Simmer 20 minutes.

Stir the cornstarch into the water and add to the zucchini. Stir until the mixture thickens. Stir in the vinegar and season to taste. Place in a hot vegetable dish to serve.

• • •

COLD MANGO PURÉE

Yield: 6 servings

4 large ripe mangoes
2 teaspoons lemon juice
1 cup plain yogurt

2 packets artificial sweetener
  or ¼ cup sugar (optional)
1 ripe kiwi

Peel the fully ripe mango fruit and cut off the flesh from the large pit. Discard both skins and pits.

Purée the mango flesh with the lemon juice in a food processor. Transfer to a bowl and fold in the yogurt. Sweeten if desired. Store in a covered bowl until ice cold. Spoon into dessert glasses and garnish each one with a slice of kiwi.

•   •   •

4
Dinner Party for Six

LEEKS VINAIGRETTE

Yield: 6 servings

18 medium leeks

Vinaigrette (page 7)

Go to a market where you can choose the leeks. They should be of medium thickness. Cut off all but one-half inch of the green part. Slit the leeks down to within one-half inch of the root. Wash very carefully in cold running water, spreading the leaves gently to remove any hidden dirt. Place in cold water and

bring to a boil. Simmer until tender (10 to 15 minutes). Drain and cool to lukewarm.

Make the vinaigrette. Just before serving, shake the vinaigrette and pour it over the leeks. This is served at room temperature as a separate course.

•   •   •

SOUFFLÉED SWORDFISH
Yield: 6 servings

2½-3 pound swordfish steak
Olive oil
3 egg whites
3 tablespoons grated Romano
   cheese

White pepper
2 tablespoons chopped
   parsley
Lemon slices

Preheat the oven for 10 minutes to 375°.

Order a steak 1¼ inches thick. Place on lightly oiled baking sheet. Brush the steak with olive oil and place it 3 inches from the broiler. Open the oven door and turn on the broiler. Broil 2 minutes.

Meanwhile beat the egg whites with a small pinch of salt until stiff. Fold in the grated cheese.

Remove the fish from the oven and with a large spatula turn it upside down onto a lightly oiled oven-proof serving platter. Spread the top with the egg white mixture and return to the oven for another 8 minutes. Sprinkle the top with chopped parsley and surround with lemon slices and Broiled Tomatoes (see next recipe).

• • •

BROILED TOMATOES

Yield: 6 servings

3 large ripe tomatoes
½ cup whole-wheat bread
   crumbs
1 large clove garlic, minced

1½ tablespoons olive oil
1 tablespoon chopped Italian
   parsley
½ teaspoon dried oregano

Wash the tomatoes. Halve them and gently squeeze out the excess juice and some of the seeds. Place them on a baking sheet.

Make a mixture of the crumbs, garlic, olive oil, parsley, and oregano and divide it among the tomatoes, spreading it over the surface of each half. Bake them in the lower third of the oven in which the swordfish is being cooked. Twelve to 15 minutes should suffice. Do not overcook or the tomatoes will lose their shape. Serve on the platter with the swordfish.

. . .

BROCCOLI WITH PESTO

Yield: 6 servings

2 pounds broccoli

½ cup Pesto (page 11)

Wash the broccoli well. Cut off all but the tender stems and divide the pieces into bite-size portions for easy serving. Place in boiling water and cook for 12 minutes. Drain thoroughly and toss in a heated vegetable dish with previously prepared pesto.

. . .

GRATIN OF MIXED FRUIT

Yield: 6 servings

3 ripe bananas
2 ripe peaches
2 ripe pears
1 lemon half

2 cups small seedless grapes
1 cup crumbled gingersnaps
1 tablespoon polyunsaturated
   margarine

Peel the bananas, peaches, and pears. Rub the fruit with the cut side of a lemon and cut into thin slices. Add 1 cup of the grapes. Chill the rest. Add the juice of ½ lemon. Arrange in a shallow ovenproof serving dish. Cover with plastic wrap and refrigerate. Crumble gingersnaps in the food processor.

To serve: Cover with the gingersnap crumbs. Dot with margarine and lightly brown under a preheated very hot broiler. Garnish with the remaining grapes. Serve warm.

"R. Hallawell . . . a party of one."

5

Dinner Party for Eight

CHILLED CUCUMBER TARRAGON SOUP

Yield: 8 servings

3 large cucumbers
4 tablespoons polyun-
    saturated margarine
4 tablespoons whole-wheat
    pastry flour
3 cups hot Chicken Broth
    (page 5)
2 cups low-fat milk
2 medium onions, chopped

1½ teaspoons chopped fresh
    tarragon or ¾ teaspoon
    dried tarragon
    Salt substitute or vegetable
    seasoning (optional)
    White pepper
1½ cups plain yogurt
    Fresh tarragon leaves for
    garnish

Peel and halve the cucumbers. Scoop out the seeds and slice the cucumbers thinly.

Melt the margarine in a skillet and sauté the cucumbers covered for 10 minutes. Stir in the flour and cook uncovered over low heat for 3 to 5 minutes. Add the hot chicken stock and stir until the mixture is thickened. At the same time, combine milk, onions, and tarragon in a small saucepan and simmer

covered over low heat for 10 minutes. Strain the milk into the cucumbers and bring to a simmer, stirring constantly. Simmer covered for 15 minutes. Purée in a food processor or blender and strain. Season to taste. Add a little green vegetable coloring if desired. Chill thoroughly. Stir in the yogurt just before serving.

To serve: Serve in bouillon cups and decorate with fresh tarragon leaves.

· · ·

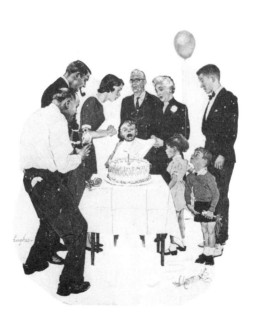

CHARCOALED CHICKEN

Yield: 8 servings

2 tablespoons chopped
   parsley
2 tablespoons tarragon
1 teaspoon chopped basil
½ teaspoon oregano
1 tablespoon scraped onion
2 teaspoons grated lemon rind

2 tablespoons honey
1 teaspoon coarse pepper
1 cup peanut oil
½ cup olive oil
¼ cup white wine vinegar
⅓ cup ketchup
2 broilers, quartered

Combine the herbs, onion, lemon rind, honey, and pepper with the oils, vinegar, and ketchup. Mix well. Wash and dry the chicken quarters. Place in an enamel-lined pot and cover the chicken with the marinade. Marinate the chicken for 24 hours, turning occasionally.

Simmer the chicken in the marinade for 30 minutes. Set aside. This may all be done in advance.

Prepare a bed of glowing charcoals and broil the chicken for 15 to 20 minutes or until nicely browned, turning the chicken pieces occasionally. Baste often with the marinade, using a bunch of parsley as a brush. Serve as befits the occasion, either mounded on a platter or on individual plates.

. . .

ALL-YEAR-ROUND CORN

*Corn picked in season fresh from the garden or corn shipped from thousands
of miles away at other times of the year tastes so good cooked this way. It
can be eaten plain, or with margarine, salt substitute and white pepper.
Corn cooked in this manner is best served as a separate course.*

Preheat the oven to 350°.

Remove the outermost leaves of 8 to 16 ears of corn, leaving on the silk and inner husk. Cut off an inch from the top and a half-inch from the bottom of each ear. Wrap each ear air-tight in aluminum foil and stack on a baking sheet. Bake 30 to 35 minutes depending on the age of the corn. Serve in the foil and supply some sort of receptacle for discarded foil and husks.

. . .

GREEN BEAN SALAD
Yield: 8 servings

1½ pounds small fresh
    green beans
2 small onions

Vinaigrette (Page 7)
12 cherry tomatoes
    Leaf lettuce

Break off the tips of the green beans and throw the beans into a small amount of boiling water. Boil for 15 to 20 minutes or until tender crisp. Meanwhile, peel and slice the onions paper thin.

Drain the beans thoroughly and toss them in ¾ cup of Vinaigrette. Cool to room temperature. Cover and store in the refrigerator.

To serve: Serve the beans on individual lettuce-lined plates or in individual lettuce-lined wooden salad bowls and dot with cherry tomato halves.

.   .   .

FRESH STRAWBERRY COMPOTE
Yield: 8 servings

3 pints ripe strawberries
4 ripe bananas

2 teaspoons lemon juice
    Plain yogurt (if desired)

Wash, hull, and halve the strawberries. Place them in a glass bowl. Shortly before serving, peel the bananas and cut them into small dice. Toss them in the

lemon juice and sprinkle over the strawberries. They will act as a sweetener for the berries. Serve the yogurt in a separate bowl for those who would like it.

.   .   .

FALL

FALL MENUS

1

Hearty Luncheon for Six to Eight

Carrot Tomato Soup
Salmon Tarragon Cake
Cornsticks
Stir-Fried Celery and Mushrooms
Baked Bananas with Orange Sauce

• • •

2

Supper for Four

Chicken-Stuffed Pasta Shells
Endive and Avocado Salad
Banana Boats

• • •

3

Dinner for Six

Chicken Breasts Dijon
Vidalia Butternut Squash
Broccoli Amandine
Party Pears

• • •

4

Dinner Party for Eight

Cucumbers in Dilled Yogurt Sauce
Chicken Thighs in Wine Vinegar Sauce
Parslied Brown Rice
Baked Spinach
Raspberry Coupé

•   •   •

5

Low-Cal Thanksgiving Dinner for Twelve

Grapefruit Cups
Poached Turkey with Low-Fat Gravy
Steamed Potatoes
Braised Onions
Glazed Turnips and Apples
Celery Platter
Three-Grain Refrigerator Rolls (page 15)
Crustless Pumpkin Pie
Fruit and Nut Bowl

•   •   •

Hearty Luncheon for Six to Eight

CARROT TOMATO SOUP

Yield: 8 servings

4 cups fresh tomatoes, peeled,
seeded, and diced or an
equal amount of drained
Italian plum tomatoes
2 pounds carrots, peeled and
sliced
3 tablespoons chopped
shallots
4 tablespoons polyun-
saturated margarine
¼ cup water

3 tablespoons whole-wheat
pastry flour
1¾ cups Chicken Broth
(page 5)
3 cups Cornstarch Milk
(page 6)
4-6 drops Tabasco
¼ cup chopped dill
1 pint yogurt
Salt substitute or vegetable
seasoning (if desired)
White pepper

Cook the tomatoes until tender.

Sauté shallots over low heat in 2 tablespoons of margarine until tender. Add
the carrots and sauté until coated with
the shallots and margarine. Add water,
and cook until the carrots are very
tender, about 30 minutes.

Heat remaining margarine in a heavy
saucepan. Whisk in the flour. Cook slowly for 2 minutes and add the chicken
broth. Whisk until thick. Combine the
carrots, tomatoes, and sauce in a food
processor and pureé until smooth. Bring
to a boil and add the cornstarch milk,
Tabasco, and two-thirds of the chopped
dill. Reheat.

Stir in the yogurt. Taste for seasoning.
Serve hot or iced, garnished with dill.

•　　　•　　　•

SALMON TARRAGON CAKE
Yield: 8 servings

1 pound boneless salmon fillet
4 teaspoons unflavored
  gelatin
½ cup cold water
½ cup light (reduced-calorie)
  mayonnaise
½ cup plain yogurt
4 ounces farmer's cheese
2 tablespoons finely chopped
  onion

1 teaspoon chopped tarragon
6 drops Tabasco
1 teaspoon salt substitute or
  vegetable seasoning
  (optional)
¼ teaspoon white pepper
1 seedless cucumber, unpared
1 teaspoon lemon juice
½ cup cream, whipped
  Tarragon leaves

Run your hand over the salmon (tail to head) to be sure there are no bones. Use a tweezer to remove any that are hidden.

Steam the salmon over boiling water in a covered pan for 10 minutes or until it flakes when pierced with a fork. Cool the salmon and chill in the refrigerator.

Soften the gelatin in the water for a minute in a small saucepan. Cook over low heat to dissolve completely, stirring frequently. Pour half of the mixture in a small bowl and the remaining half into a larger bowl. Cool to room temperature.

Flake the salmon with your fingers. There should be about 1½ cups. Stir 4 tablespoons each of the mayonnaise and yogurt into the larger bowl. Add 1 tablespoon of the onion, the Tabasco, ½ teaspoon of salt substitute, ⅛ teaspoon pepper, and the lemon juice. Mix well and add the salmon. Place in the refrigerator. Stir occasionally.

Add the remaining mayonnaise, yogurt, the cheese, onion, and salt substitute to the smaller bowl and whisk until blended. Wash and cut the cucumber in half. Chop one half quite fine. Drain well. Add the cucumber and the chopped tarragon to the mayonnaise mixture. Stir well and taste for seasoning. Refrigerate. Stir both mixtures every 5 minutes for about 20 minutes or until the mixtures are thickened.

Whip the cream to soft peaks and fold half of it into each bowl. Spread half of the salmon mixture into an 8-inch springmold or straight-sided 2-quart souffle mold. Smooth the top evenly and cover with all the cucumber mixture. Cover with the remaining salmon mixture, smoothing it evenly. Cover with plastic wrap and refrigerate overnight.

To serve: Cut the rest of the cucumber in thin slices. Unmold the cake onto a serving platter. Surround with small leaves of garden lettuce. Decorate the top with cucumber slices and tarragon leaves.

•   •   •

CORNSTICKS
Yield: 12 servings

1 cup all-purpose flour
1 cup high-lysine cornmeal
2 teaspoons sugar
4 teaspoons baking powder
2 eggs, lightly beaten, or
    egg substitute

½ cup yogurt
½ cup low-fat milk
2 tablespoons polyun-
    saturated margarine,
    melted
2 tablespoons safflower oil

Preheat the oven to 400°.

Vegetable-spray the cornstick molds (or 2½-inch muffin pans) generously. Place in oven for five minutes or until sizzling hot.

Combine all the dry ingredients in one bowl and all the wet ingredients in another. Combine the two and mix until smooth.

Fill the pans two-thirds full and bake 12 to 15 minutes (3 minutes longer for muffins). Remove from the pan and stack them on a serving plate.

• • •

STIR-FRIED CELERY AND MUSHROOMS
Yield: 8 servings

4 cups prepared celery
1 pound mushrooms
4 tablespoons sesame or
    peanut oil

1 tablespoon chopped parsley
2 teaspoons lemon juice

Trim the leaves from well-washed celery. Cut stalks diagonally into 1½-inch pieces. If the celery is not tender, throw it into boiling water and boil 1 minute. Drain and dry.

Slice the mushrooms.

Heat a wok or skillet and add the oil. When the oil is very hot, add the celery pieces. Stir-fry 2 to 3 minutes, tossing continually. Add the mushrooms and continue to stir-fry for 2 minutes.

Sprinkle with parsley and lemon juice and toss a moment longer. Serve immediately.

• • •

BAKED BANANAS WITH ORANGE SAUCE
Yield: 8 servings

8 small bananas
2 tablespoons melted
   polyunsaturated margarine
1½ teaspoons grated orange
   rind
½ teaspoon grated lemon rind
2 tablespoons orange juice
2 tablespoons honey

Orange Sauce
1 tablespoon cornstarch
1 cup water
2 tablespoons maple syrup
2 tablespoons polyun-
   saturated margarine
   Grated rind of 1 orange
¼ cup orange juice
2 teaspoons lemon juice

Preheat the oven to 375°.

Rub with margarine a shallow dessert platter.

Peel the bananas and cut them in half. Place the banana halves in the dessert platter in a decorative fashion. Brush them with the remaining margarine. Grate the rinds and squeeze the juice from 1 orange and 1 lemon into separate containers.

Combine the orange and lemon rinds with the 2 tablespoons of orange juice and 1 teaspoon of lemon juice and 2 tablespoons of honey. Mix well. Spoon the mixture over the bananas. Bake 5 to 10 minutes, or until the honey bubbles.

To make the sauce, stir the cornstarch into the cold water in the top of a double boiler. When blended, add the maple syrup and cook over boiling water for 10 minutes. Remove from the heat. Stir in the margarine, orange rind, orange juice, and lemon juice. Serve lukewarm.

•   •   •

Supper for Four

CHICKEN-STUFFED PASTA SHELLS
Yield: 4 servings

40 jumbo pasta shells

Quick Tomato Sauce
½ **cup chopped onion**
2 **tablespoons olive oil**
2 **cloves garlic, pressed**
1 **pint tomato puree**
1 **bay leaf**
¼ **teaspoon powdered thyme**
½ **teaspoon vegetable seasoning or salt substitute
   (optional)**
⅛ **teaspoon white pepper**

Filling:
2 **tablespoons polyun-
   saturated margarine**
½ **pound fresh mushrooms,
   sliced thin**
½ **pound low-fat cottage
   cheese, well drained**
2 **cups cooked chicken,
   chopped fine**
⅔ **cup grated Parmesan
   cheese**
1 **tablespoon egg substitute**

Bring a large kettle of water to a boil. Add the shells and bring back to a boil over high heat. Boil 10 minutes or until tender but not mushy. Drain, freshen in cold water, drain again and line up in single layer on a baking sheet.

At the same time, start the tomato sauce. Sauté the chopped onion in the olive oil without letting it brown. When soft, add the garlic, the tomato pureé, the bay leaf, thyme, and seasonings and simmer uncovered 30 minutes. Remove the bay leaf.

Heat the margarine in a skillet and saute the mushrooms for 2 minutes. Remove from the heat and stir in ⅓ cup of

the cottage cheese, the chopped chicken, and ⅓ cup of the Parmesan cheese. Stir in the egg substitute and mix well. Fill the shells with the mixture, using either a teaspoon or a pastry bag fitted with a plain tip.

Place half the filled shells in the bottom of a lightly oiled oven-proof serving dish.

Stir the remaining cottage cheese into the tomato sauce, and pour half of it and half the remaining Parmesan cheese over the filled shells. Fill with the rest of the shells and cover with the rest of the sauce and cheese. Bake in a preheated 375° oven for 20 minutes.

• • •

ENDIVE AVOCADO SALAD

Yield: 4 servings

3 Belgian endives
1 avocado
½ lemon

½ recipe Creamy Herb
  Dressing (page 10)
2 black olives
  Leaf lettuce

Remove the ends of the endives and break them carefully into individual leaves. Cut the large leaves in half. Place in a bowl of ice water to crisp.

Peel the avocado and cut in half lengthwise. Rub the halves with the cut side of a lemon.

Just before serving, drain the endives and pat dry with paper toweling. Place in a bowl. Slice the avocado into the bowl and toss lightly with the dressing. Serve in individual salad bowls lined with lettuce leaves and garnish with a pitted olive half to give an accent to the salad.

• • •

BANANA BOATS
Yield: 4 servings

Children will enjoy helping to prepare this dessert.

4 firm but ripe bananas
½ lemon
2 small sweet tangerines or
   Clementines

2 kiwis
   Slivered almonds
1 large sweet orange, squeezed
   Garnish: raisins, dried
      apricots, cherries, etc.

Cut an eighth of an inch off the outer curved side of the banana so that it will sit on a plate. Cut off the top half of the peel and the very top of the banana so that you have a smooth surface. Cut all around the edge with a very thin sharp knife and cut the banana into half-inch sections and remove about every fourth section. Rub the exposed banana with the cut side of the lemon to keep it from darkening.

Peel the tangerines and kiwis. Divide or cut them into sections. Remove all possible fiber from the tangerines. Insert the kiwis and tangerines alternately between the banana sections. Slip the slivered almonds all around the edge between the banana and the skin. Garnish as you will, making a gondolier of raisins on a toothpick or a lady passenger with an apricot picture hat. Spoon a little orange juice over the fruit for added sweetness.

• • •

3

Dinner for Six

CHICKEN BREASTS DIJON

Yield: 6 servings

6 chicken breasts, (6 to 8
    ounces each) skinned
    and boned
1 teaspoon marjoram
1 teaspoon dried thyme
½ cup unbleached wheat flour
1 teaspoon freshly ground
    pepper
1 teaspoon grated lemon rind
8 thin lemon slices

4 tablespoons polyun-
    saturated margarine
    Watercress
2 tablespoons peanut oil
1 cup tomato juice
1 pint Chicken Broth
    (page 5)
2 tablespoons Dijon mustard
⅔ cup Cornstarch Milk
    (page 6)

Halve the chicken breasts and lay them out on a piece of wax paper. Cover with a sheet of wax paper and pound them with the side of a large cleaver or other flat object until they are ¼ inch thick.

Measure ¼ teaspoon of each herb into a bowl.

Mix the flour, remaining herbs and pepper and spread it on a plate. Reserve 1½ tablespoons of the mixture. Coat the chicken breasts with the rest.

Grate the lemon rind. Cut the lemon into 8 thin slices. Cut the slices in half without cutting all the way through.

Heat the margarine and oil in a large heavy skillet and, when it sizzles, cook the chicken breasts for 2 minutes. Turn and cook 2 minutes longer. Transfer the chicken to a platter or shallow casserole dish. Add the tomato juice to the pan and stir the mixture to incorporate all the juices. Cook for 5 minutes or until thickened. Add the broth, mustard, and lemon rind. Boil 2 minutes.

Add the reserved herbs to the cornstarch milk. Pour the milk into the hot sauce and stir over low heat until thickened. Taste for seasoning. Add the chicken pieces and reheat, spooning the sauce over the chicken. If made in advance, reheat starting from room temperature for 30 minutes in a 300° oven.

To serve: Arrange the chicken pieces on a platter. Top each piece with a twisted slice of lemon and garnish with watercress.

•   •   •

VIDALIA BUTTERNUT SQUASH
Yield: 6 servings

Vidalia onions are particularly sweet and flavorful and are becoming quite common in the supermarket. Substitute scallions if not available.

3 pounds butternut squash
¼ cup chopped Vidalia onions
3 tablespoons polyun-
    saturated margarine
1-1½ cups Chicken Broth (page 5)

⅛ teaspoon freshly grated
    nutmeg
    Salt substitute or vegetable
    seasoning (optional)
    White pepper
1 tablespoon chopped parsley

Wash the squash well. Cut in chunks, removing the seeds and fibers from the bulb. Steam peeled or unpeeled (as you prefer) for 20 to 25 minutes or until tender.

Heat 1½ tablespoons of the margarine in a small skillet. Stir in the onions and cover. Cook over very low heat for 20 minutes, stirring occasionally. Do not let the onions brown.

Drain the squash and remove the skin, if not previously peeled. Put the pulp in mixing bowl and beat with an electric mixer until smooth. Add the remaining margarine and seasonings as desired. Beat in enough broth to give a smooth thick consistency. Mix in the onions and place in a serving dish. Sprinkle the top with chopped parsley.

·   ·   ·

BROCCOLI AMANDINE
Yield: 6 servings

2 bunches broccoli
⅓ cup Chicken Broth (page 5)
3 tablespoons polyun-
    saturated margarine
4 tablespoons fine whole-
    wheat breadcrumbs

4 tablespoons finely chopped
    almonds
¼ teaspoon white pepper
    Salt substitute or vegetable
    seasoning (optional)
2 tablespoons chopped parsley

Cut off all the thick woody stalks from the broccoli and cut into flowerets. Cook in boiling water just until tender. Do not overcook. Drain thoroughly.

Vegetable-spray a shallow baking/serving dish and arrange the flowerets attractively in the dish. Spoon the broth over the broccoli.

Heat the margarine and brown the crumbs and nuts in the margarine. Sprinkle over the surface of the broccoli. Season with pepper and salt substitute if desired. Reheat in a 300° oven for 25 to 30 minutes. Garnish with the chopped parsley just before serving.

·   ·   ·

PARTY PEARS
Yield: 6 servings

3 Anjou pears, firm but ripe
½ lemon
2 tablespoons polyun-
  saturated margarine
2 tablespoons sugar

Honey Cheese Cream
(page 14)
Garnish: cloves and mint
  leaves

Peel and halve the pears. Scoop out the core with a spoon. Rub each half with the cut side of a lemon. Place cut side down on a lightly vegetable-sprayed baking sheet. Draw pretty designs on the pears with the tip of a sharp knife, incising them about ¼-inch deep. Brush with melted margarine and sprinkle each one with a teaspoon of sugar.

Just before serving, place the pears under a preheated broiler. Grill until the sugar carmelizes lightly.

Pour the Honey Cheese Cream in a shallow dessert platter. Arrange the pears on top and serve. Garnish each one with a clove and a mint leaf.

4
Dinner Party for Eight

CUCUMBERS IN DILLED YOGURT CREAM
Yield: 8 servings

2 long seedless cucumbers
Boiling water
1 pint plain yogurt
4 tablespoons cider vinegar
2 teaspoons honey
½ cup sliced green onions

1 tablespoon snipped dill
Salt substitute or vegetable
seasoning (optional)
½ teaspoon white pepper
Fresh dill

Slice the cucumbers very thin using a sharp knife or a food processor slicer. Place in a bowl. Pour boiling water over the cucumbers and let stand 2 minutes. Drain and transfer to a bowl of ice water. Let stand 15 minutes. Drain and pat dry with a towel.

Meanwhile mix the yogurt, cider vinegar, and honey until well blended. Add the onions, dill, and seasonings. Stir in the cucumbers. Cover and refrigerate for at least 1 hour. Arrange in a shallow dish and garnish with fresh dill.

•   •   •

CHICKEN THIGHS IN WINE VINEGAR SAUCE
Yield: 8 servings

8 chicken thighs, skinned
1 tablespoon polyunsaturated
margarine
10-15 cloves garlic, unpeeled
¾ cup red wine vinegar
2 ripe tomatoes or ⅔ cup
drained Italian plum
tomatoes
1 tablespoon tomato paste

Pepper
Bouquet garni
1½ cups hot Chicken Broth
(page 5)
4 tablespoons unsalted polyunsaturated margarine,
cut in small pieces
Italian parsley

Heat the margarine in a skillet. Brown the thighs well on both sides, turning them with pincers. Add the unpeeled garlic cloves. Cook covered over low heat for 20 minutes. Holding the cover slightly ajar, pour off most of the grease. Add the wine vinegar to the pan. Boil uncovered for about 10 minutes or until the liquid is almost syrupy. Add the tomatoes, the tomato paste, pepper, and the bouquet garni. Simmer 10 minutes. Remove the chicken from the pan and

keep warm. Add the broth and boil down until the sauce is rich and concentrated. Force through a strainer, pressing hard on the garlic.

Reheat the sauce to the boiling point, remove from the heat and whisk in the margarine in small pieces. Arrange the chicken on a platter. Pour over part of the sauce and decorate with a few sprigs of parsley. Serve the rest of the sauce in a separate bowl.

•   •   •

PARSLIED BROWN RICE
Yield: 8 servings

6 quarts water
2 cups brown rice
4 tablespoons polyun-
    saturated margarine

¼ cup chopped parsley
    Salt substitute or vegetable
    seasoning (optional)
Black pepper

Bring the water to a boil in a large kettle. Add the rice gradually so that the water never stops boiling. Boil for 40 to 45 minutes, until the rice is tender but not mushy. Drain in a colander and put in a serving bowl. Add the margarine and fluff the rice with 2 forks. Add the parsley and seasonings to taste and fluff again.

If it is more convenient to cook the rice in advance, cool it and store it in the refrigerator before seasoning. Before serving, cover and reheat in a 300° oven for 25 minutes. Toss with the margarine, parsley, and seasonings just before serving.

•   •   •

BAKED SPINACH
Yield: 8 servings

3 pounds fresh-picked spinach
    or 3 boxes frozen spinach
2 tablespoons polyun-
    saturated margarine
1 cup farmer's cheese

1 cup thick Cornstarch Milk
    (page 6)
1 teaspoon lemon juice
⅛ teaspoon nutmeg
    Salt substitute (optional)
    and pepper

If using fresh spinach, wash in several waters and remove any tough stems. Lift the spinach from the water into a large kettle. Cover and cook 5 to 6 minutes or until tender. Drain in a large colander.

Place frozen spinach in a heavy kettle. Add 1 cup of water. Place over high heat and break up the spinach with a fork. Bring to a boil and cook 3 minutes. Drain and press out all excess moisture.

Place the spinach in a food processor. Add the margarine, cheese, cornstarch milk, and lemon juice. Season with salt substitute, pepper, and nutmeg. Puree until smooth. Place in a 1½-quart lightly greased baking/serving dish. If made in advance, cool, cover, and refrigerate. If you do not have a large food processor, do this in two batches.

About 25 minutes before serving, place in a preheated 300° oven. Allow 5 minutes extra if the spinach has been chilled.

•   •   •

RASPBERRY COUPÉ
Yield: 8-10 servings

This is also very good made with strawberries.

2 quarts fresh raspberries
1 pint freshly squeezed
   orange juice

1 teaspoon lemon juice
4 tablespoons maraschino
   cherry juice

Wash and hull the raspberries. Place in a glass bowl. Squeeze the orange juice and add the lemon and cherry juice. Pour over the fruit gently. Do not stir.

Cover with plastic wrap and chill in the refrigerator for 2 to 3 hours. Serve in individual bowls.

•   •   •

Low-Cal Thanksgiving Dinner for Twelve

GRAPEFRUIT CUPS
Yield: 12 servings

6 medium-size grapefruit
6 large navel oranges
1 large bunch small seedless
   red grapes
1 can (16 oz.) pineapple tidbits, packed in pineapple
   juice

3 McIntosh apples
2 tablespoons lemon juice
2 packages artificial
   sweetener (optional)
12 mint leaves

Cut off a very thin slice at each end of the grapefruit so that the halves will sit evenly on the plate. Cut the grapefruit in half in a shallow plate so that the juices can be caught. Remove the seeds. Spoon out the grapefruit sections with a fruit spoon. Cut out all the white filaments, using kitchen scissors. Notch the edges for a decorative effect. Cover and refrigerate.

Halve the oranges and remove the seeds. Spoon out the sections and squeeze out any juice. Discard the skins and filaments.

Cut the grapes in half if large. Peel the apples and cut into bite-size pieces. Drain the pineapple tidbits. Mix the orange, grapefruit, apples, and pineapple.

Strain and combine the juices in a measuring cup and add the lemon juice and sweetener, if desired. Pour a little over the fruit. Cover and refrigerate the fruit, and the rest of the juice separately.

To Serve: Fill the grapefruit cups with the fruit and place on individual plates. Add as much of the juice as possible without running over. Garnish each cup with a mint leaf and bring them to the table before inviting people to the table.

•   •   •

POACHED TURKEY WITH LOW-FAT GRAVY
Yield: 12-14 servings

*Everyone likes the Norman Rockwell version of an American Thanksgiving
or Christmas dinner when the platter is brought in from the kitchen with the huge
roast turkey garlanded and bedecked, to be carved and served with mounds of mashed
potatoes and large servings of luscious fat-filled gravy. Unfortunately, such a feast
can undo weeks of careful eating for those who are watching fat and salt in their diets,
so there must be an alternative. The alternative has one great advantage—it is
prepared a day in advance. In fact, most of the meal is prepared
a day or two in advance, making life much easier for the cook.*

1 14-pound turkey, cut in quarters	1 cup chopped onion
3 tablespoons cider vinegar	1 cup finely sliced celery
1 large onion	1 cup finely chopped carrots
2 cloves	2 large cloves garlic, finely minced
6 peppercorns	¾ cup cornstarch
3 stalks celery	Kitchen Bouquet
1 large carrot, cut in pieces	Pepper
1 large bay leaf	Vegetable seasoning or salt substitute (optional)
1 teaspoon dried thyme	

One or two days in advance: Ask the butcher to cut a fresh turkey into quarters. Remove the skin, where most of the fat resides, from the bird. Place the meat in a kettle. Add the vinegar, the large onion stuck with the cloves and whole peppercorns, the celery, and carrots, bay leaf, thyme, and enough water to come to the top of the meat. Bring to a boil. Cover and simmer for 1½ hours. Remove the white meat, and if the dark meat is not tender give it 15 minutes longer. Remove the dark meat. Boil down the cooking liquid by half and strain it. Discard vegetables and bay leaf. Cool and chill the broth so that all the fat will rise to the top. Wrap the cooled meat carefully to prevent it drying out and refrigerate.

Measure out 2½ quarts of the defatted broth. Bring 2 quarts to a boil and add the shredded vegetables and garlic. Cook partially covered for 30 minutes. The vegetables will slightly thicken the sauce. Mix the remaining 2 cups cold defatted broth with the cornstarch. Remove the boiling mixture from the heat and gradually add the cornstarch mixture, whisking to avoid lumping. Simmer the mixture for 8 minutes over low heat, stirring frequently until quite thick. Color with a few drops of Kitchen Bouquet. Season as desired.

To serve: Pour a little of the sauce in the bottom of a shallow platter. Slice both dark and white meat diagonally in fairly thick slices and lay them decoratively on the sauce. Surround with steamed white potatoes and sprinkle with chopped parsley. Serve the rest of the sauce in a separate bowl.

•   •   •

STEAMED POTATOES
Yield: 6 servings

12 medium-size potatoes   **Italian parsley**

Wash the potatoes well, but do not peel them unless you want to for the sake of appearance. Place in a steamer basket and place the basket in its kettle holding 3 to 4 inches of water. Bring to a boil and steam for 20 to 25 minutes or until the potato is tender when pierced with a sharp knife. Place around the edge of the turkey platter and garnish each one with an Italian parsley leaf.

• • •

DeBellis

BRAISED ONIONS
Yield: 12 servings

24-36 small onions
3 tablespoons polyun-
  saturated margarine
Defatted chicken or turkey
  broth

Vegetable seasoning or salt
  substitute (optional)
White pepper
2 tablespoons chopped
  pimiento

Peel the small onions. Heat the margarine in a large skillet and toss the onions in the margarine until lightly browned on all sides. Shake the pan or stir frequently. Remove the onions with a slotted spoon to a heatproof serving dish. Add enough broth to come halfway up the side of the onions. Cover and bake at 375° until all the liquid has been absorbed and the onions are tender.

Season with vegetable seasoning or salt substitute, if desired, and white pepper. Sprinkle with the chopped pimiento.

• • •

GLAZED TURNIPS AND APPLES
Yield: 12 servings

3 pounds white turnips
6 Cortland or Granny Smith
   apples
4 tablespoons polyun-
   saturated margarine
   Vegetable seasoning or salt
   substitute (optional)

Paprika
2 tablespoons brown sugar
1 cup defatted turkey or beef
   broth
   Chopped parsley

Peel and cut the turnips into ¼-inch slices. Boil in hot water for 10 minutes. Drain thoroughly and pat dry with toweling.

Peel, core, and cut the apples crosswise into ¼-inch slices. Cut them in half if easier to handle.

Heat the margarine in a large nonstick skillet until very hot. Add the turnips and apples and brown them on all sides, turning them with a plastic spatula. Transfer to a heatproof serving dish. Discard the margarine. Sprinkle with vegetable seasoning or salt substitute, if desired, the paprika and sugar, and pour the broth around the edges. Bake uncovered at 375° until all the moisture has disappeared and the surface is slightly shiny. Sprinkle with chopped parsley. Serve from the dish.

•   •   •

CELERY PLATTER

Celery hearts
Pitted green olives packed
   in water

2 large carrots (room
   temperature)
Cherry tomatoes

Wash the celery. Remove the outside stalks and divide the centers into individual stalks with the little leaves left on. Put them in a small plastic bag. Cut the larger stalks into narrow 3-inch strips and make little bundles of 4 or 5 of the thin strips. Thread the strips through the olives. Put in a plastic bag. Refrigerate everything until serving time.

Wash and peel the carrots. Trim one side so that you can lay the carrot down on a surface. Using a swivel vegetable peeler, make long thin flat strips. This will take a little practice. Roll up the strips and fasten them with a toothpick. Put them in a bowl of ice water and refrigerate.

Wash the cherry tomatoes but do not remove the stems.

To serve: Place the filled olives down the center of a small platter. Surround with the tender inner stalks. Remove the toothpicks from the carrot curls and place them between the filled olives and the celery stalks alternately with the cherry tomatoes.

CRUSTLESS PUMPKIN PIE

Yield: 12 servings

*Thanksgiving without pumpkin pie just isn't Thanksgiving, but
the traditional pumpkin pie is sky-high in calories and other no-nos. This
facsimile supplies the taste and even the appearance.*

2 eggs
1 egg yolk
1 can (16 ounces) pumpkin
½ cup granulated maple sugar
   or ½ cup granulated sugar
   and ½ teaspoon pure maple
   flavoring
1½ cups low-fat milk
½ teaspoon freshly ground
   nutmeg

½ teaspoon ginger
1 teaspoon cinnamon

Topping:
   Whipped Dessert Topping
   (page 14)
2 tablespoons diced candied
   ginger
12 pecan halves

Preheat the oven to 350°.

Vegetable-spray a 10-inch pie plate.
Beat the eggs and egg yolk until light.
Add the pumpkin and beat until thoroughly blended. Add the maple sugar,
low-fat milk, and spices and continue
beating until well mixed. Pour into the
prepared pan. Place on a baking sheet
and bake on the center rack for 50 minutes or until a knife inserted halfway
towards the center comes out clean. Do
not overbake. Cool and then chill.

To serve: Using a pastry tube, pipe the
whipped topping around the edge of the
pie. Sprinkle with the diced ginger.
Place the pecan halves in the centers of
what will be the 12 sections the "pie" is
cut into.

•   •   •

FRUIT AND NUT BOWL

A fruit and nut bowl is reminiscent of
early Colonial days in the South when
all the dishes and the dinner cloth were
removed after a long repast, and the
fruit bowl was brought in for guests to
enjoy along with post-prandial conversation for as long as they wanted to linger.

Remove the floral centerpiece from the
center of the table and replace it with a
beautifully arranged bowl of fruit. Try
not to repeat any of the fruits that have
been eaten during the meal, and concentrate on the late summer and fall fruits
such as apples, pears, apricots, plums,
grapes of many varieties and even a few
bananas, as well as walnuts, hickory
nuts, pecans, almonds, and Brazil nuts.
Plates and fruit knives are all you need
for utensils.

Coffee or tea served with this makes it
a special occasion.

•   •   •

WINTER

WINTER MENUS

1

Luncheon for Four to Six

Vegetarian Whole-Wheat Crepe Cake
Cherry Tomatoes Fines Herbes
Light Raspberry Mousses

. . .

2

Lunch or Supper for Six

Herbed Spaghetti Ring
Tomato Artichoke Aspics with Saga Sauce
Black Olive High-Lysine Cornmeal Muffins
Oatmeal Apricot Squares

. . .

3

Dinner for Four

Baked Scallops
Creamy Beets
Cauliflower and Broccoli Platter
Prune Walnut Whip

. . .

4

Supper for Four

Cod Packages
Fresh Pea Pureé
Coleslaw
Spiced McIntosh Applesauce

. . .

5

Dinner for Six

Mushroom Boats
French Eggplant Cake
Peach Yogurt Melba

. . .

6

Dinner for Ten to Twelve

Rolled Turkey Breast, Alsatian Style
Orzo Gratin
Carrot Tarragon Purée
Apricots in Orange Juice

. . .

7

Buffet Supper for Eight to Ten

Buffet Chicken Salad
Elegant Fish Paté
French Tomato Salad
Lentil Salad
Tortellini and Broccoli Salad
Celeriac Salad
Individual Whole-Wheat Pizzas
Strawberry Cream Bombe

. . .

1

Luncheon for Four to Six

VEGETARIAN WHOLE-WHEAT CREPE CAKE
Yield: 4-6 servings

This dish is a meal in itself. It is a recipe with many parts, all of which can be prepared a day in advance. The cake can be assembled three or four hours before serving. Allow 2½ hours for baking.

18 Whole-Wheat Crepes
(page 12)

Filling:
2 pounds fresh broccoli or
1 box (10 ounces) frozen
chopped broccoli, thawed
1 pound carrots
3 tablespoons polyun-
saturated margarine
Vegetable seasoning
2 tablespoons chopped parsley
1 pound mushrooms
2 teaspoons lemon juice
½ teaspoon salt substitute
(optional)
1 cup shredded low-sodium
Swiss cheese

2 teaspoons Dijon mustard
4 tablespoons chopped green
onions
⅛ teaspoon mace

Low-Fat Cheese Custard:
1 cup farmer's cheese,
thoroughly drained
3 egg substitutes
1 cup Cornstarch Milk
(page 6)
Vegetable seasoning
⅛ teaspoon white pepper
⅛ teaspoon mace

Simple Tomato Sauce
(page 11)

If using fresh broccoli, remove all the coarse stems leaving the flowerets. Cook in boiling water for 10 to 12 minutes or until tender-crisp. Drain and rinse in cold water. Drain again.

Thaw frozen broccoli in a colander.

Make the crepes according to directions. Set aside.

Filling: Scrub the carrots very clean, or, if necessary, scrape off the skin with a potato peeler. Cut into thin rounds by hand or with a food processor slicer. Put them in a pan of cold water. Bring to a boil and cook for 5 minutes. Drain well and toss in a bowl with 1 tablespoon of margarine, 1 teaspoon of lemon juice and the chopped parsley.

Brush the mushrooms clean and chop them and the green onions briefly in a food processor. Sauté gently in 1 table-spoon of margarine until the mushrooms are almost dry. Toss or stir frequently. Season with salt substitute, if desired, white pepper, and 1 teaspoon of lemon juice. Set aside.

Shred the Swiss cheese. Mix with the mustard and green onions.

Toss the broccoli in 1 tablespoon of margarine and season to taste with lemon juice, white pepper, and a pinch of mace. Set aside.

Beat the farmer's cheese, egg substitute and cornstarch milk until very smooth, using an electric hand mixer or a food processor. Season to taste with white pepper, mace, and vegetable seasoning.

Make the tomato sauce.

To assemble the cake: Preheat the oven to 350°.

Lightly oil or vegetable-spray the bottom and sides of a 6-cup deep, straight-sided soufflé dish or Charlotte mold. Line the bottom with a circle of parchment or wax paper. Lightly oil the paper and cover it with two crepes. Line the sides of the pan with overlapping crepes. Spread the bottom crepe with ¼ cup of the shredded cheese and mustard mixture. Cover with the carrots and add ⅓ of the custard mixture. Cover with 2 crepes and spread them with the mush-rooms. Add another third of the custard and cover with another crepe. Spread half of the remaining cheese/mustard mixture over the crepes and cover with the broccoli. Spread with the final third of the cheese/mustard mixture and the rest of the custard. Fold in the tops of the crepes lining the pan and cover with 2 or 3 more crepes. Place a lightly oiled piece of parchment or wax paper on top of the crepes and cover the pan with aluminum foil. Place on the middle rack in the oven and bake 1 hour. Turn the heat up to 400° and bake 1 hour longer.

Unmold on a platter and garnish with a sprig of parsley. Surround the base with a ring of tomato sauce and serve the rest in a separate bowl. The cake is cut in wedges like a pie.

. . .

"You eat too fast."

81

CHERRY TOMATOES FINES HERBES
Yield: 8 servings

1 quart cherry tomatoes
3 cloves garlic, minced
2 tablespoons chopped basil
2 tablespoons chopped
    parsley

¼ cup olive oil
2 teaspoons lemon juice
½ teaspoon salt substitute or
    vegetable seasoning (op-
    tional)

Wash and stem the tomatoes. Cut them in half.

Press the garlic and chop the herbs quite fine.

Toss the tomatoes with the garlic, oil, lemon juice, and optional seasonings. Just before serving stir in chopped herbs.

•   •   •

LIGHT RASPBERRY MOUSSES
Yield: 6 servings

1 pint low-fat cottage cheese
1 pint fresh raspberries
1½ packages plain gelatin
4 tablespoons water

4 tablespoons raw honey
1 tablespoon lemon juice
8 mint leaves

The night before you make this, put the cottage cheese in a strainer over a bowl and let it drain overnight into the bowl.

At the same time crush 1 cup of the raspberries by hand or with a food processor and strain them to remove the seeds. Save the rest for garnish.

The next morning stir the gelatin into the water. Heat the honey in a small saucepan. Add the gelatin and cook over low heat until the gelatin is completely dissolved. Cool to lukewarm.

Combine the gelatin/honey mixture and lemon juice with the strained cottage cheese and raspberry purée. Mix well and pack into individual dessert dishes. Chill until firm.

To serve: Scatter raspberries over the surface of each serving. Garnish each with a mint leaf.

•   •   •

Lunch or Supper for Six

HERBED SPAGHETTI RING

Yield: 8 servings

1 pound whole-wheat
    spaghetti
1 pound mushrooms
3 tablespoons polyun-
    saturated margarine
2 eggs, slightly beaten
3 tablespoons chopped chives

2 tablespoons chopped
    parsley
3 tablespoons flour
2 cups Chicken Broth
    (page 5)
    Salt substitute or vegetable
    seasoning (optional)
¼ teaspoon white pepper

Cook the spaghetti in rapidly boiling water until tender (12 to 14 minutes, depending on thickness of spaghetti). Drain and run cool water over the spaghetti, tossing to separate. Drain again.

Trim the mushrooms. Wash very briefly and chop coarsely in the food processor or by hand. Heat the margarine in a skillet and sauté the mushrooms over high heat for 3 minutes. Add the chives and parsley and cook gently 2 to 3 minutes longer. Stir in the flour and when that disappears, add the chicken broth. Cook and stir until the mixture thickens. Remove from the heat and stir in the beaten eggs gradually, beating constantly. Finally, add the cooked spaghetti. Season to taste. Fill a large well-oiled ring mold with the spaghetti mixture.

Place the ring mold in a pan of hot water and bake 50 minutes at 350°. To test for doneness, insert a thin knife. If it comes out clean the ring is cooked. Invert onto a round warm platter. Cut in wedges to serve.

If cooking this in advance, cook the spaghetti and rinse in cold water. Prepare the mushroom sauce but do not combine them. One hour before serving, stir the sauce well, combine with the spaghetti, and bake.

•   •   •

TOMATO ARTICHOKE ASPICS WITH SAGA SAUCE
Yield: 8 servings

3¾ cups unseasoned tomato
  juice
2 tablespoons gelatin
2 teaspoons lemon juice
1 teaspoon horseradish
2 teaspoons reduced-sodium
  soy sauce
1 jar (6 ounces) artichoke
  hearts

Saga Sauce:
1 pint plain yogurt
3 ounces Saga cheese
  Juice of 1 lemon
  Salt substitute or vegetable
  seasoning (optional)
¼ teaspoon freshly ground
  pepper
  Lettuce

Bring 1 cup of tomato juice to a boil.
Soften the gelatin in ¼ cup of cool
tomato juice and add to the boiling tomato juice. Stir until completely dissolved. Add to the remaining juice and
stir in the lemon juice, horseradish, and
soy sauce.

Pour ¼ inch of the tomato mixture into
each of 8 large nonstick muffin tins.
Chill in the refrigerator until firm.

Drain the artichokes, saving the vinaigrette. Cut each heart in half and divide
the hearts among the muffin tins and
fill the tins with the remaining aspic.
Chill 2 to 3 hours in the refrigerator.

Meanwhile make the sauce: Crumble the
cheese into the yogurt and mix well.
Add the remaining ingredients and mix
well. Chill in the refrigerator.

To serve: Turn the aspics upside down
on a tray or baking sheet. Line individual salad plates with leaves of garden
lettuce. Spread a little of the reserved
vinaigrette on each leaf. Using a spatula, transfer an aspic to each plate and
cover with the Saga Sauce.

•   •   •

BLACK OLIVE HIGH-LYSINE CORNMEAL MUFFINS
Yield: 12 large muffins

1 small can (3¼ ounces) water-
 packed sliced black olives
1 cup unbleached all-purpose
 flour
1 cup high-lysine cornmeal
1 tablespoon baking powder
1 large egg or egg substitute

½ cup olive liquid
½ cup low-fat milk
6 drops Tabasco
3 tablespoons polyun-
 saturated unsalted
 margarine, melted

Preheat the oven to 400°.

Open the can of olives and drain off the liquid.

Combine the flour, cornmeal, and baking powder in one bowl and mix them well.

Beat the egg until frothy. Add the olive liquid, the milk, the Tabasco, sliced olives, and melted margarine. Stir into the dry ingredients just until the dry ingredients are moistened. Let stand 5 minutes.

Lightly oil 12 large nonstick muffin tins. Fill the tins two-thirds full with the batter. Bake 25 minutes.

. . .

OATMEAL APRICOT SQUARES
Yield: 6-8 servings

2 cups oatmeal
½ cup brown sugar
5 tablespoons polyun-
 saturated margarine (room
 temperature)

1½ cups unsulphured apricots
2 tablespoons honey

Make a mixture of the oatmeal, brown sugar, and margarine, and knead it by hand until well mixed. Press two-thirds of the mixture into an ungreased 8x8-inch pan.

Cook the apricots and water over medium-low heat until the apricots are tender. Purée in a food processor. Cool

slightly and stir in the honey. Spread over the oatmeal base. Cover with the remaining oatmeal mixture and bake 30 to 35 minutes in a preheated 350° oven. Cool to lukewarm and cut into squares. If desired, garnish each with a small portion of low-calorie whipped topping and top with a small section of dried apricot.

. . .

3
Dinner for Four

BAKED SCALLOPS
Yield: 4 servings

1 pound sea or bay scallops
2 tablespoons polyun-
    saturated margarine
½ cup whole-wheat cracker
    crumbs

1 tablespoon lemon juice
1 tablespoon chopped dill

Sea scallops should be cut in quarters or thirds depending on size. Bay scallops are left whole. Spray a skillet with vegetable spray. Heat the skillet and add the margarine. As soon as it bubbles, add the cracker crumbs. Mix quickly and remove from the stove. Add the scallops and toss or stir just until they are coated on all sides. Transfer to a shallow baking dish. Sprinkle with lemon juice. Cover and refrigerate until 20 minutes before serving. Bake uncovered in a preheated 350° oven for 20 minutes and sprinkle with chopped dill.

• • •

CREAMY BEETS
Yield: 4 servings

1 pound can sliced beets
    Cream Sauce (page 7)
1½ teaspoons cider vinegar

½ teaspoon dried dill
    Fresh dill (optional)
    White pepper

Drain the juice of canned beets into a saucepan. Add the vinegar and dried dill and cook down to 4 tablespoons. Place the sliced beets in an oven- or microwave-proof serving dish.

Make the cream sauce, but do not add the lemon juice. Season to taste with white pepper.

Combine the sauce and reduced beet juice. Pour over the beets and reheat just before serving. Garnish with fresh dill if desired.

• • •

"Waiter, there's a hook in my soup."

CAULIFLOWER AND BROCCOLI PLATTER
Yield: 4 servings

1½ pounds fresh cauliflower
1 pound fresh broccoli
2 tablespoons polyun-
   saturated margarine
2 tablespoons blanched
   almonds
4 medium cherry tomatoes

1 tablespoon Dijon mustard
½ tablespoon chopped dill
   Pinch cardamom seed
1 tablespoon water
   Freshly ground black
   pepper

Cut off the thick stems from the cauliflower and broccoli, leaving just the flowerets.

Halve the tomatoes. Toast the almonds under a preheated broiler. Watch carefully to be sure they do not burn. Set aside.

Sauté the cherry tomatoes in 1 teaspoon of heated margarine in a small skillet just until they are heated through. Transfer to a small dish. Cover and keep warm.

Heat the remaining margarine in the same skillet until it bubbles. Remove from the heat and stir in the mustard, water, cardamom, and pepper. Keep in the skillet for quick reheating.

At the same time fill 2 large saucepans half full with water and bring to a boil. Boil the broccoli 3 minutes. Boil the cauliflower 5 minutes. Both vegetables should be tender-crisp. Drain each vegetable separately. Drain thoroughly.

Arrange the broccoli around the edge of a small heated platter. Pile the cauliflower in the center. Sprinkle the almonds over the cauliflower and pour the reheated sauce over both. Arrange the tomato halves decoratively between the two vegetables and garnish with the dill.

If you have a microwave you can arrange the vegetables on the platter in advance and reheat, covered loosely with wax paper, for 2 to 3 minutes (from room temperature). Pour over the reheated sauce and add the almonds just before serving.

•   •   •

PRUNE WALNUT WHIP

Yield: 4 servings

1 cup (well-packed) naturally
    dried prunes
½ stick cinnamon
2 tablespoons sugar

2 teaspoons lemon juice
⅓ cup chopped walnuts
3 egg whites, beaten stiff
    Artificial sweetener
    (optional)

Put the prunes in a saucepan. Add the cinnamon, sugar, and just enough water to barely cover the prunes. Bring to a boil and cook 8 minutes. Remove the cinnamon stick and pureé the prunes in a food processor until smooth. Put the pureé back in the saucepan and stir over heat until the pureé is very thick. Remove from the stove and transfer to a bowl. Add the lemon juice and the walnuts. Cool to lukewarm.

Preheat the oven to 400°. Place in it a baking dish with 1 or 2 inches of water.

Beat the egg whites until they reach the soft-peak stage—not too dry. Fold a third of the egg whites into the prune pureé and stir well. Fold in the remaining egg whites gently and pile into 4 individual soufflé dishes. Place them in the dish of hot water in the oven. The water should come halfway up the sides of the dishes. Bake 15 or 20 minutes; they should be firm. Serve warm or cold. Sprinkle on a little sweetener if desired.

· · ·

Supper for Four

COD PACKAGES

Yield: 4 servings

1 head Romaine lettuce
4 fresh cod fillets (about
    4 ounces each)
2 teaspoons chopped onions
1 tablespoon chopped carrots
1 tablespoon chopped celery
¾ cup water
1 tablespoon lemon juice

Vegetable seasoning
White pepper
8 ounces evaporated skim
    milk
1 teaspoon margarine
2 teaspoons unbleached
    wheat flour

Choose a large head of Romaine and carefully remove the outer leaves. Wash four leaves well and cut out the main white rib. Dip into boiling water for a few seconds and then plunge into cold water. Lay out on a working surface and trim and shape as needed to make a wrapping.

Ask your fish dealer for fillets without skin or bones. Place a fillet in the center of each lettuce leaf. Wrap the lettuce around the fillets so that they are completely enclosed. Place in a pan just large enough to accommodate the packages. Sprinkle the chopped vegetables over the top. Combine water and lemon juice. Add ½ cup of water and season with vegetable seasoning and white pepper.

Cover and simmer for 4 to 5 minutes depending on the thickness of the fillets. Meanwhile mix the margarine and flour into a paste. Transfer the packages to a warm platter, leaving the vegetables in the sauce. Turn up the heat, add the remaining water/lemon juice, and boil down the sauce to about ½ cup. Add the evaporated milk. When the mixture boils, add the paste in small bits, whisking constantly to thicken the sauce. Taste for seasoning and pour over the packages. Serve with plain steamed potatoes.

•   •   •

FRESH PEA PURÉE

Yield: 4 servings

3 pounds fresh peas
2 tablespoons polyun-
    saturated margarine
2 shallots, minced

4-5 tablespoons skim milk
    Vegetable seasoning
    White pepper

Shell the peas. Drop them into boiling water and cook 8 minutes or until just tender.

Meanwhile heat the margarine in a saucepan. Add the shallots and cover. Cook over very low heat until tender. Do not allow to brown. Remove from the heat.

Drain the peas and freshen in cold water. Drain again. Place in the food processor and purée with the skim milk, adding more milk if necessary. Add the purée to the shallots and stir well until the mixture is very hot. Season to taste with vegetable seasoning and white pepper. Serve very hot.

• • •

QUINTANAR

COLESLAW

Yield: 4 servings

1½ pounds cabbage
1 Vidalia onion

1 recipe Boiled Salad
    Dressing (page 11)

Slice the cabbage into fine shreds using a sharp knife or a food processor. Slice the onion as thin as possible and divide into rings. Alternate layers of cabbage and onions in a large bowl. Cover with ice water and let stand for at least 1 hour.

Drain the cabbage and onions thoroughly and pat dry with a towel. Toss with the boiled dressing. Serve very cold.

• • •

SPICED McINTOSH APPLESAUCE

Yield: 4 servings

McIntosh apples may not be the most flavorful of apples, but they are very sweet and demand little or no extra sweetening. Add a little artificial sweetener, if desired.

1½ pounds McIntosh apples
⅛ teaspoon cinnamon
Dash of cloves
¼ teaspoon ginger

⅛ teaspoon nutmeg
4 tablespoons chopped walnuts
4 tablespoons golden raisins
Low-fat yogurt (optional)

Wash the apples and core them, but do not peel them. Cover with water. Cook covered until tender. Drain and force through a food mill. Add the cinnamon, cloves, ginger, nutmeg, walnuts, and raisins and cool to lukewarm. Serve lukewarm or chilled, plain or with yogurt.

· · ·

Dinner for Six

MUSHROOM BOATS
Yield: 6 servings

*The markets are selling a wide variety of mushrooms these days which
have much more flavor than the common white mushroom. Try this recipe with
any of them, or if you know mushrooms well, pick your own.*

6 whole-wheat French rolls
1 tablespoon polyunsaturated
   margarine, melted
1 pound oyster or other
   variety of mushrooms
2 shallots, minced
3 tablespoons polyun-
   saturated margarine

3 tablespoons whole-wheat
   pastry flour
¾ cup Chicken Broth (page 5)
⅛ teaspoon nutmeg
½ lemon
⅛ teaspoon pepper
¾ cup plain yogurt
   Italian parsley

Cut the top of a long side of each roll
out and remove the interior crumb, thus
making a little basket. Brush the insides
lightly with the melted margarine and
heat in a low oven while preparing the
filling. Brush clean the mushrooms. Set
aside 6 caps or, if the mushrooms are
large, save 3 and cut them in half. Chop
the remainder quite coarsely. Heat 1
tablespoon of margarine in a skillet.

Sauté the chopped mushrooms and the
shallots together until the mushrooms
are almost dry. Remove to a bowl.

Sauté the caps briefly on both sides and
remove to a small plate. Add the remaining 2 tablespoons margarine and
heat until melted. Whisk in the flour.
Whisk until thick. Season with nutmeg,
pepper, and lemon juice. (Save the
lemon skin and cut it into 6 thin slices
to form basket handles, discarding any
bits of fruit.)

Reheat the chopped mushrooms in the
sauce. Add the yogurt but do not allow
to boil. Fill the baskets with the mushroom mixture. Put the "handles" in
place and garnish with a mushroom cap
and a piece of parsley.

•   •   •

FRENCH EGGPLANT CAKE

Yield: 6 servings

1 pound ripe but firm tomatoes	3 cloves garlic (optional but recommended)
1 large shallot	1 teaspoon dried mint
2 long eggplants (not too large)	Olive oil
1½ pounds small zucchini	Peanut oil
2 medium onions	Salt substitute and pepper
	Bunch of mint

Peel, halve, and seed the tomatoes. Cut them into medium dice. Chop the shallot very fine and sauté over low heat in 1 tablespoon of oil until tender. Add the tomatoes and cook down until all the moisture has disappeared.

Meanwhile, wash, trim, and peel the eggplant in long strips and save the skins. Cut the flesh in slices lengthwise. Peel and mince the garlic if desired. Peel and chop the onions very fine. Wash and dice the zucchini.

Heat 1 inch of peanut oil in a deep skillet. Sauté several of the eggplant slices until browned on both sides. Transfer with a slotted ladle to a paper towel-lined baking sheet to drain. Repeat until all the slices are browned. Using the same skillet, brown the zucchini dice. Remove with a slotted ladle to another towel-lined tray to drain off any oil.

Heat 3 tablespoons of olive oil in another skillet and sauté the garlic and onions until just tender. Season with salt substitute and pepper. Add the chopped mint and the sautéed zucchini. Stir and cook 5 minutes.

Cut the reserved eggplant skins into long narrow strips and cook in boiling water for 1 minute. Drain well.

Lightly spread margarine into a 9-inch spring mold. Line the bottom with a circle of parchment paper. Arrange the eggplant strips, lattice fashion, on the bottom and sides with the shiny side down. Line the entire mold with eggplant slices. Fill with the zucchini mixture, packing it in tightly. Place the mold in a pan of hot water and bake for 25 minutes at 375°.

Unmold the eggplant in the center of a round, heated platter. Fill the lattice spaces with the diced tomatoes and garnish with mint leaves.

• • •

"Lay off the fast food. You're getting too McFat."

PEACH YOGURT MELBA
Yield: 6 servings

1 package (10 ounces) frozen
   raspberries, thawed
2 teaspoons cornstarch
2 tablespoons cold water
1 teaspoon lemon juice
   Mint leaves (optional)

6 peach halves canned in
   their own juice
1 pint lemon yogurt
   Artificial sweetener
   (optional)

Put portions of the lemon yogurt in the bottoms of individual dessert glasses. Top with the peach halves, cut side down. Spoon on the raspberries, dividing them among the six glasses. Top with the remaining yogurt and refrigerate. Serve garnished with mint leaves.

If the lemon yogurt seems too tart for your taste, you may sprinkle a little artificial sweetener over the tops.

•   •   •

Dinner for Ten to Twelve

ROLLED TURKEY BREAST, ALSATIAN STYLE
Yield: 10-12 servings

This is a festive party dish and worth the effort.

5 pound boned turkey
   breast, butterflied

Stuffing:
5 tablespoons polyun-
   saturated margarine
1 cup chopped onion
8 Cortland apples
½ teaspoon cinnamon
¼ cup apple juice
½ teaspoon sage
3 cups whole-wheat bread-
   crumbs

1 can (6¾ ounces) sliced water
   chestnuts
1 teaspoon vegetable
   seasoning
   Freshly ground black pepper
2½ cups apple juice
1½ cups Chicken Broth
   (page 5)
1 cup plain yogurt
2 tablespoons chopped
   parsley

Order the turkey breast. Ask the butcher to butterfly the breast so that you have a long piece, roughly rectangular in shape. Have him score the flesh and pound it to a ½- to ¼-inch thickness. to see that there are no holes in the flesh or skin. If you do not have an obliging butcher, spread the boned turkey out on a working surface. If the butcher has not butterflied it, cut the very fleshy sides in half, starting in the center on both sides, running the knife parallel to the skin but not all the way through so that you can fold it out, thus lengthening the breast. Score the flesh with a sharp pointed knife. Place between two long pieces of wax paper and pound with a heavy cleaver or other flat-bottomed object until it measures the proper thickness.

Heat 2 tablespoons of the margarine in a skillet. Stir in the chopped onion. Cover and cook over low heat for 10 minutes, stirring occasionally. Do not brown.

Peel, quarter, and core the apples. Cut the quarters into thin sections. Heat 2 tablespoons of the margarine in another skillet. Sauté a few sections at a time in the hot margarine. They should be lightly browned and just tender. Transfer to a dish with a slotted spoon. Continue until all the apples are cooked. Sprinkle the apples with the cinnamon and ¼ cup apple juice. Combine the onions, apples, sage, breadcrumbs, and water chestnuts. Let the stuffing cool completely.

Season the turkey breast with vegetable seasoning and freshly ground black pepper. Spread the stuffing over the turkey breast, leaving a margin of 1 inch on the outside edges. Put any extra stuffing in a small casserole. Roll up and bind with butcher's twine. Paint the surface with a tablespoon of melted margarine. Roast in a long roasting pan or jelly roll pan, seam side down. Add 1½ cups of apple juice and the chicken broth to the pan. Cover the ends of the turkey roll with aluminum foil on which you have rubbed a little margarine.

Roast 2 hours in a preheated 350° oven, basting every 15 minutes with the pan juices. Remove the foil. Baste well and roast 20 minutes longer. Transfer the roast to a long platter and keep warm. Pour one cup of apple juice into the pan, to deglaze it. Bring to a boil and cook 3 minutes. Remove from the heat and stir in the yogurt and chopped parsley. Heat but do not boil. Pour into a separate gravy boat.

To serve: Remove the twine from the roll. Pour a little of the sauce over the roast. Garnish with parsley sprigs and onion chrysanthemums.

Onion Chrysanthemums: Choose medium-size round onions. Peel them and slice them from the top all around the onion in thin slices down to within ½ inch from the root end. Place the onion in a bowl of boiling water for 5 minutes. The flower will start to open its petals. Then place in a bowl of ice water tinted with whatever food coloring you please. Transfer to a paper towel to dry. If you wish, insert a thin carrot stick in the center to serve as a stamen.

• • •

ORZO GRATIN
Yield: 10-12 servings

1 pound orzo (rice-like pasta)
8 cloves garlic
1 cup Cornstarch Milk
  (page 6)
  or light cream
1 cup Chicken Broth (page ??)
1 cup freshly grated
  Parmesan cheese
1 cup Mushroom Duxelles
  (page 12)
1 cup minced parsley
6 tablespoons dry whole-
  wheat breadcrumbs
2 tablespoons cold polyunsaturated margarine

Boil the orzo and the unpeeled garlic in a large kettle of boiling water for 10 minutes or until the pasta is just tender. Drain in a colander and run cold water through it. Drain again. Prepare the Duxelles.

Pick out the garlic cloves and remove the peel. Mash the garlic in the bottom of a mixing bowl. Stir in the cornstarch milk or light cream. Add the orzo, the broth, ½ cup of Parmesan, the Duxelles and ½ cup of chopped parsley. Season with pepper and mix well. Spoon into a lightly oiled baking/serving dish.

Mix the breadcrumbs and remaining cheese and spread evenly over the orzo. Dot with the margarine broken into small pieces. Bake 1 hour and 15 minutes in a preheated 325° oven.

• • •

CARROT TARRAGON PUREÉ
Yield: 10-12 servings

This can be made in advance and reheated.

8 cups sliced carrots
2 cups diced raw potatoes
3-4 slices fresh lemon
½ teaspoon dried tarragon
5-6 tablespoons margarine
1½ cups low-fat cottage cheese

¼-½ cup thick Cornstarch Milk
(page 6)
Powdered vegetable
seasoning (optional)
¼ teaspoon white pepper
Fresh tarragon leaves

Put the carrots and potatoes in a saucepan and cover them with water. Add the lemon and the tarragon. Bring to a boil and cook until tender, 12 to 15 minutes. Drain well and purée with a food blender or food mill. Add the margarine, cottage cheese, vegetable seasoning, if desired, and pepper. Pour in gradually a small amount of cornstarch milk, for smoothness. Pile into a vegetable dish and swirl the top with a knife. Garnish the top with fresh tarragon leaves.

. . .

APRICOTS IN ORANGE JUICE
Yield: 10-12 servings

2 pounds unsulphured dried
apricots

2 tablespoons lemon juice
1 quart freshly squeezed
orange juice

Put the apricots in a glass serving bowl. Cover them with the orange and lemon juice. Let stand covered in the refrigerator for 2 days. Serve in individual dessert dishes.

. . .

7

Buffet Supper for Eight to Ten

BUFFET CHICKEN SALAD
Yield: 8-10 servings

2 whole chicken breasts
8 tarragon leaves
4 cups potato cubes
1 package frozen mixed
  vegetables, thawed
⅔ cup Vinaigrette (page 7)
1 tablespoon capers
1 cup chopped celery
½ cup chopped scallions

1 large clove garlic, pressed
  Freshly ground black pepper
2 tablespoons chopped parsley
  Vegetable seasoning or salt
  substitute
  Roasted pimiento
⅓ cup light (reduced-calorie)
  mayonnaise

Remove the skin from the chicken breasts. Rub very lightly with olive oil and place 2 tarragon leaves on each breast. Line a small roasting pan with aluminum foil. Lay the breasts upright on the foil and cover loosely but air-tight with a tent of foil, thus allowing air to circulate so that the breasts will cook evenly. Bake 1 hour and 15 minutes at 350° and test for doneness with a meat thermometer. Bake a little longer if necessary. Cool and then chill before carving.

Meanwhile prepare the salad. Peel the potatoes and cut them into ¾-inch dice. Boil in water for 10 to 12 minutes or until tender. Drain thoroughly and mix with the thawed vegetables. Toss with the vinaigrette while still hot. Add

the capers, scallions, celery, garlic, parsley, pepper and vegetable seasoning or salt substitute, if desired. Cover and let stand at room temperature for at least an hour. Pack tightly into a shallow round pan, pouring off any excess dressing.

Cut out pretty shapes of roasted pimiento for future decoration.

To serve: Unmold the salad onto a round serving platter. Spread a film of mayonnaise over the surface. Slice the chicken breasts thin enough to be cut with a fork and place them in a spiral shape all over the surface of the salad. Garnish the edge with the pimiento and sprinkle chopped parsley over the chicken spiral.

•   •   •

ELEGANT FISH PATÉ
Yield: 8 servings

1½ pounds fresh whitefish
    fillets
    Salt substitute and white
    pepper
⅔ cup water
1 stick polyunsaturated
    margarine, divided
1 tablespoon chopped shallot
2 quarts water
2 cups tightly packed spinach
    leaves
2 eggs
1½ pounds fresh salmon fillet
4 teaspoons lemon juice

Chive Mayonnaise:
1 cup light (reduced-calorie)
    mayonnaise
½ cup yogurt
2 teaspoons lemon juice
4 tablespoons chopped chives
    or scallion tops

Garnish:
    Sliced cucumbers and
    chopped parsley

Preheat the oven to 275°.

Oil a 2-quart casserole or 8-cup loaf pan.

Cut 8 ounces of the whitefish fillets into thin strips 2 inches long and ½ inch wide. Place the strips in a glass dish. Sprinkle with salt substitute and pepper and pour the water mixed with 2 teaspoons of lemon juice over them.

Heat two tablespoons of margarine in a small skillet. Add the shallots and stir until coated. Cover and cook over low heat 4 or 5 minutes or until tender. Do not allow to brown. Set aside.

Remove the stems from the spinach leaves. Bring the water to a boil and add the spinach leaves. Cook 1 minute. Drain, pressing out all excess moisture. Pureé in the food processor. Set aside.

Separate the egg whites from the yolks.

Pureé the remaining whitefish fillets just until smooth. Add the egg whites and 2 tablespoons of margarine and 2 teaspoons of the cooked shallot. Season with a little salt substitute and white pepper. Process just until blended. Mix one-third of the mixture with the spinach. Place the rest of the pureé in a bowl.

Pureé the salmon in the food processor. Add the egg yolk, remaining 2 teaspoons of lemon juice, remaining shallot, and 2 tablespoons of margarine. Process until blended.

Drain the fish strips.

Spread half the salmon mixture in the bottom of the loaf tin. Cover with half of the fish strips. Cover with half of the whitefish mixture, then with the spinach mixture, then with the other half of the fish mixture and then the other half of the fish strips. Cover with the remaining salmon.

Cover with a double thickness of aluminum foil and place in a roasting pan half full of water. Bake 2 hours. Remove from the roasting pan and cool completely. Refrigerate overnight.

Make the Chive Mayonnaise by combining the ingredients.

To serve: Unmold on a long platter. "Frost" the top with some of the Chive Mayonnaise and garnish with cucumber slices sprinkled with chopped parsley.

. . .

FRENCH TOMATO SALAD
Yield: 8-10 servings

8-10 large ripe firm tomatoes
1 tablespoon minced garlic
⅔ cup Vinaigrette (page 7)
1½ tablespoons chopped
    parsley

1 tablespoon chopped basil
    (optional)
Salt substitute or vegetable
    seasoning (optional)

The tomatoes can be dipped in hot water and peeled in advance if more convenient. Do not slice until shortly before serving.

Chop the garlic, parsley, and basil and keep in separate small containers. Cover and refrigerate unless you are near serving time.

Just before serving, slice the tomatoes into a bowl. Sprinkle with the garlic and vinaigrette. Toss lightly and season to taste as desired. Sprinkle the surface with the chopped parsley and basil. Serve with whole-wheat French bread.

. . .

100

LENTIL SALAD
Yield: 8-10 servings

2 cups dried green lentils
2 small onions, sliced thin
½ cup Vinaigrette (page 7)

2 large cloves garlic
2 tablespoons chopped
    parsley

Soak the lentils overnight. Remove any that float to the top. Cover with 1 quart water and cook until tender. (Processed lentils take 20 minutes. Regular lentils take 90 minutes.) Drain thoroughly.

Slice the onions very thin and divide into rings. Press the garlic. Mix the warm lentils with the Vinaigrette, onions, and garlic. Cover and let stand at least 30 minutes. Spread in a shallow platter and sprinkle with chopped parsley.

. . .

TORTELLINI AND BROCCOLI SALAD

Yield: 8-10 servings

*Tortellini are stuffed with a very light cheese mixture and are used
most often as a garnish for soup, but they also make a delicious salad. Mixed
with broccoli, they make a colorful addition to a buffet supper.*

8-ounce bag frozen cheese-
 stuffed tortellini
Several strips lemon rind

1 bunch broccoli
¾ cup Vinaigrette (page 7)
3 tablespoons Parmesan
 cheese

Simmer the tortellini in water flavored with lemon rind for 10 minutes or until just tender. Drain.

At the same time, cut off the flowerets of the broccoli, separating each small bunch. Cook in boiling water 8 to 10 minutes or just until tender. Drain.

While still warm, toss the broccoli and tortellini together with the Vinaigrette. Serve at room temperature. Toss with the Parmesan just before serving.

.   .   .

CELERIAC SALAD

Yield: 8-10 servings

*Celeriac, often called celery root, is a member of the parsnip family
that is becoming popular in America. The favorite way to serve it is as a crisp
crunchy salad, but it appears sometimes as a first course and sometimes as a part of
the buffet. It is a brown, round, rather unattractive-looking root vegetable
that has to be peeled and trimmed, and often goes unnoticed in the
market, but it is delicious when properly prepared.*

2-3 celeriac (according to size)
1 tablespoon white wine
 vinegar
2 teaspoons lemon juice
2 tablespoons Dijon mustard
 Commercial "light"
 mayonnaise

Freshly ground pepper
Vegetable seasoning or salt
 substitute (optional)
2 tablespoons chopped
 parsley
1 tablespoon chopped chives

Peel the rough skin from the celeriac. Cut the flesh in thin slices and then into thin match sticks. (This can also be done in a large food processor.) Put in a non-metal bowl and toss with vinegar. Cover and let stand 30 minutes. Rinse in cold water and drain thoroughly. Mix with the lemon juice, mustard, pepper, and enough mayonnaise to moisten. Taste and add other seasoning if needed. Refrigerate for several hours. Serve in a bowl, sprinkled with a mixture of the chopped parsley and chives.

.   .   .

INDIVIDUAL WHOLE-WHEAT PIZZAS
Yield: 4 pizzas

Lo-Chol Pastry (page 14)
Simple Tomato Sauce
  (page 11)
3 ounces skim-milk mozzarella
½ pound mushrooms
4 pinches oregano

Vegetable seasoning or salt
  substitute (optional)
2 teaspoons olive oil
8-10 pitted black imported olives
  or 8-10 anchovy fillets,
  washed (optional)

Make the pastry following directions on page 14. Roll out ¼ inch thick and cut into four 6-inch circles. Vegetable-spray four 5-inch foil or tin pie pans. Press the dough into the pans. Chill 1 hour in the freezer.

Bake 8 minutes at 400°. Remove from the tins when cool enough to handle and place on a cool baking sheet.

Filling: Prepare the tomato sauce, cooking it down until quite thick. Do not allow it to scorch. Set aside to cool.

Slice the mozzarella and the mushrooms very thin.

To fill and bake: Brush each pizza shell very lightly with olive oil. Spread a layer of tomato sauce in each pizza. Cover with slices of mozarella and then with the mushrooms. Sprinkle with oregano and vegetable seasoning, if desired. Let stand.

Preheat the oven to 400°.

Just before baking, sprinkle the top with Parmesan and dribble ½ teaspoon of olive oil over each one. Bake 20 to 25 minutes. Just before serving, dot with the black olives that have been pitted and cut in half, and place the anchovy strips (that have been washed to remove the salt) on the surface.

Cut each pizza into 6 wedges so that they can be easily served.

•   •   •

STRAWBERRY CREAM BOMBÉ

Yield: 10-12 servings

3 pounds low-fat cottage
   cheese
2 packages frozen sliced
   strawberries

1 pint fresh whole
   strawberries

Put all the cottage cheese in a colander and let it drain for an hour. Discard the liquid. Place a plate on top of the cheese and weight it with a heavy object. Place over a small round tray and refrigerate overnight.

Thaw the sliced strawberries.

Wash but do not hull the fresh strawberries.

To serve: Unmold the cheese on a dessert platter. Cover with the thawed strawberries and garnish with the whole strawberries.

•   •   •

RECIPE INDEX